An Amish Family Christmas

Center Point
Large Print

Also by Shelley Shepard Gray and available from Center Point Large Print:

Thankful
Joyful
The Promise of Palm Grove
The Proposal at Siesta Key
A Wedding at the Orange Blossom Inn
A Christmas Bride in Pinecraft
A Son's Vow
A Daughter's Dream
The Loyal Heart
A Sister's Wish

An Amish Family Christmas

A Charmed Amish Life Christmas Novel

SHELLEY SHEPARD GRAY

Center Point Large Print
Thorndike, Maine

This Center Point Large Print edition is published
in the year 2016 by arrangement with Avon Inspire,
an imprint of HarperCollins Publishers.

This is a work of fiction. Names, characters, places, and incidents are products of the author's imagination or are used fictitiously and are not to be construed as real. Any resemblance to actual events, locales, organizations, or persons, living or dead, is entirely coincidental.

The text of this Large Print edition is unabridged.
In other aspects, this book may vary from the original edition.
Printed in the United States of America on permanent paper.
Set in 16-point Times New Roman type.

ISBN: 978-1-68324-201-7

Library of Congress Cataloging-in-Publication Data

Names: Gray, Shelley Shepard, author.
Title: Center Point Large Print edition. | An Amish family Christmas : a charmed Amish life Christmas novel / Shelley Shepard Gray.
Description: Thorndike, Maine : Center Point Large Print, 2016.
Identifiers: LCCN 2016040397 | ISBN 9781683242017
(hardcover : alk. paper)
Subjects: LCSH: Amish—Fiction. | Large type books. | Christmas stories. | GSAFD: Christian fiction.
Classification: LCC PS3607.R3966 A84 2016 | DDC 813/.6—dc23
LC record available at https://lccn.loc.gov/2016040397

To Alex,
the newest member of our family

Acknowledgments

As I finish up this novel, I wanted to be sure to thank some of the many people who have helped me make this Charmed Amish Life Series the best that it could be.

First off are Lynne and Laurie. Thank you to "Team L&L" for driving with me to Charm and exploring the area. No fried-pie tasting would be complete without you! Thank you both for the thousand things y'all do to help make my writing life go smoothly. Thank you for being so patient and fun, too. Y'all are awesome. Really!

Thank you to the whole team at HarperCollins and Avon Books! No author could be more spoiled! I am grateful for the beautiful covers, the marketing and sales teams, the enthusiasm, and most of all for their kindness to me. I owe Amelia Wood and Maria Silva special thanks for jumping on board with the marketing and publicity for this series. Both of these ladies are so smart and talented! Thank you, also, to editor Chelsey Emmelhainz for planning out this series with me (and listening patiently while I continually chatted about all things Amish and Charm) and to the lovely Erika Tsang, who has recently adopted me. I'm grateful for all of you!

I owe a big thanks to everyone at the Seymour Agency, and most especially Nicole Resciniti. Nicole, thank you for being there for me in hundreds of ways this year. I've been humbled and honored to call you my agent.

Writing four books a year means I work a lot, and I'm so grateful for my husband, Tom. He takes care of everything (everything except laundry!). He not only understands when I have to work long hours, but also notifies me when it's time for a break.

Finally, I want to give thanks to the Lord for helping me write each page. I am so grateful I don't have to write these books on my own. I'm blessed.

Will you rejoice in the birth of the King?
Or just in the things Christmas will bring?

AMISH PROVERB

"What do you mean, 'if I can?' Jesus asked.
"Anything is possible if a person believes."

MARK 9:23

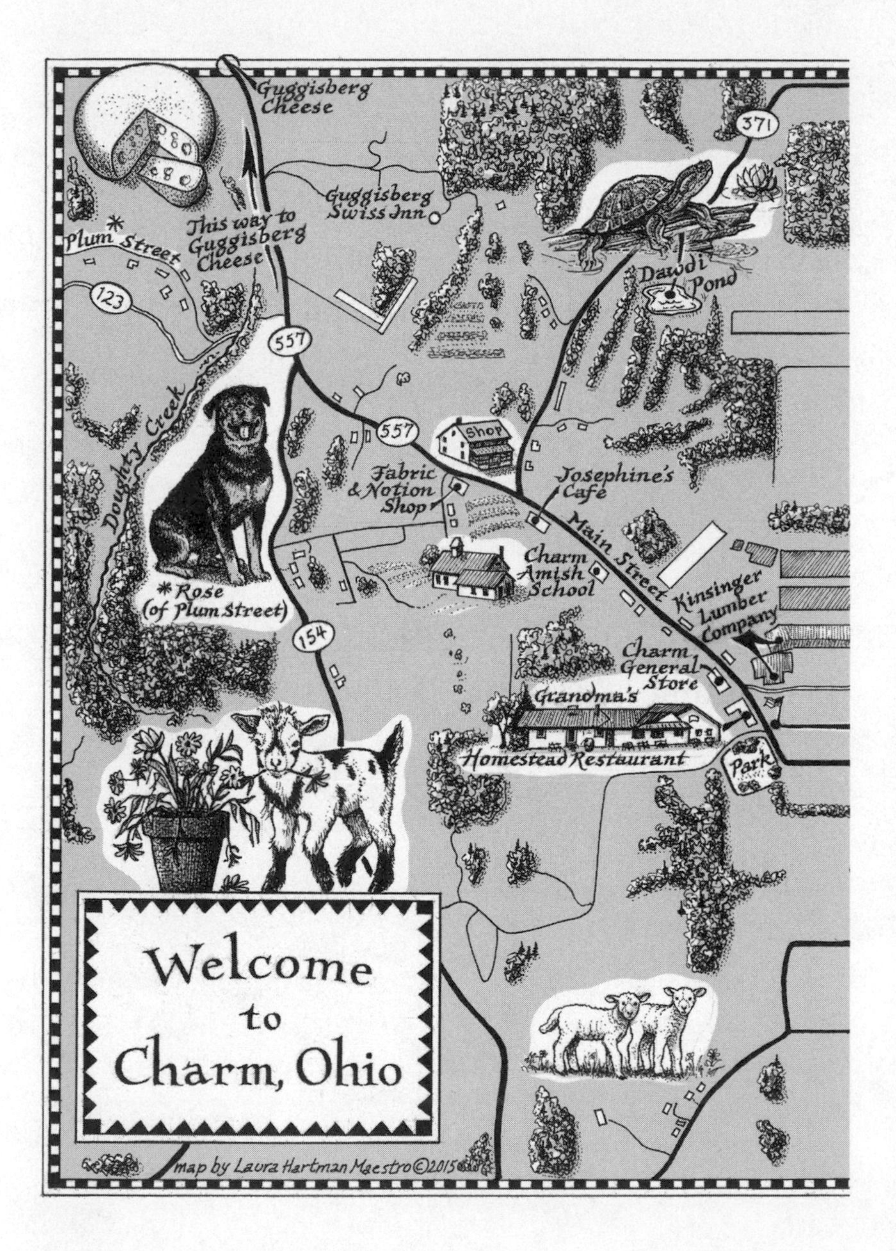
Guggisberg Cheese
This way to Guggisberg Cheese
Guggisberg Swiss Inn
Plum Street
123
557
371
Dawdi Pond
Doughty Creek
Shop
Fabric & Notion Shop
Josephine's Cafe
Main Street
Charm Amish School
Kinsinger Lumber Company
Rose (of Plum Street)
154
Charm General Store
Grandma's Homestead Restaurant
Park
Welcome to Charm, Ohio
map by Laura Hartman Maestro ©2015

371
369
157
The Kinsinger Home
Oscar
Simon's House
159
Charm Public School
Bank
70
U.S. Post Office
557
600
Darla's Farm
Walnut Creek
Many of these locations are real, but like Princess the goat and Oscar the bulldog, Shelley imagined a few, too.

Chapter 1

❄ ❄ ❄

December 3

"Momma, it's cold."

"It is, for sure," Julia Kemp murmured to her daughter. Frustrated, she jiggled the handle of her front door for about the fifteenth time. Standing on her porch, she debated about whether or not to dump out the contents of her purse and tote bag. Again.

The temperature had to be hovering around the twenty-degree mark. Far too cold for a five-year-old to be outside for any length of time. Then, of course, there was the foot of snow that had fallen over the last two days. While it was beautiful, it also seemed to keep the moisture firmly in the air. Now it felt even colder than it actually was.

Feeling both helpless and annoyed with herself, Julia pulled off her black cardigan and slipped it around Penny's little body. "There you are, dear. Better?"

Penny bit her lip but nodded bravely. She was already snuggled in Julia's coat and her own cloak, *kapp*, and black bonnet. Actually, she was a little hard to see, nestled in the pile of clothes like a newborn pup.

But now that she had her mother's sweater tucked securely around her, Penny had to be all right. It was most likely the situation they were in that was making her feel so chilled and scared.

And who could blame her? They were locked out of their house at eight at night on December third. There was snow on the ground, not a streetlight to be seen, and everyone around them was a virtual stranger. Nothing about their current situation was okay.

Somehow, some way, she'd lost her house keys. How could she do something so stupid? So dumb?

Just as that old familiar sinking feeling of unworthiness started to threaten her very being, she shook her head. No, she was not going to do this to herself again.

She was not going to put herself down like Luther used to do. She was not stupid. She was not dumb. She'd merely made a mistake, that was all. People made mistakes all the time.

But as the wind blew and the bitter cold seeped through the wool fabric of her dress, Julia knew it was time to face the inevitable. She didn't know any of her neighbors well enough to feel like she could ask for help, especially when it meant that she would have to ask Penny to trudge up and down a dark street in the snow. She was going to have to break into her house tonight. Penny needed to get into bed and get her rest. She had school tomorrow.

There was no other choice.

Hoping she sounded more optimistic than she felt, Julia knelt down and pressed her lips to her sweet girl's soft cheek. "Penny, I'm going to need to look around the yard for a rock. You stay here, okay?"

"Why do ya need a rock?"

"Because I'm going to have to break one of the windows so we can get inside the house."

Caramel-colored eyes that matched her own gazed at her solemnly. "Okay, Momma."

That was how her little girl answered her most all the time now. She accepted whatever Julia told her without a fuss. And no matter what happened, she tried to keep up a brave front.

Tears pricked Julia's eyes as she stepped off the front porch and wandered into her small front lawn. She had no idea where she was going to find a rock under all the snow in the dark, but she had to try.

She was not going to think about how one went about getting a new windowpane or how much it was going to cost. Or how her small bank account was going to be able to pay for it. All she needed to do was take things one day at a time. Or, in this case, one hour at a time.

She could do this. She had been making do for

the last six years, ever since she'd allowed Luther liberties he shouldn't have taken and then discovered the consequences.

Still remembering that awful afternoon, she shivered. She'd been scared but hopeful that Luther would eventually be the kind man to her in private that he was to her family in public. Instead, he'd called her terrible names and hit her. When she realized she was pregnant, she knew he would never let her go. Instead of facing her parents and confessing everything, she ran. She'd been too embarrassed to admit her many faults, especially since her sister Sarah had done everything right.

In addition, her parents didn't believe in conflict or dissent. Julia had been sure that they would have been upset that she'd slept with a man she didn't want to marry. Maybe even upset enough to force her to stay by Luther's side.

Letting those fears consume her, she'd hired a driver to take her from Middlefield to Cleveland. Then, after spending the night in a scary motel near the downtown bus station, she boarded a bus bound for Millersburg.

By the time she'd walked into a small, quaint-looking motel just off the highway that had a Help Wanted sign in the front window, she'd had a new identity.

She was Julia Kemp, widow. Her husband had been killed in a construction accident, and she'd moved to Ohio to start over on her own. The baby she was expecting was a blessing.

And her swollen eye? She'd tripped while managing her suitcase in the bus station.

Jared and Connie Knepp, owners of the motel, had accepted her sad story without blinking an eye. And Julia had gotten a small room the size of a large closet and a job cleaning rooms. For almost six years she'd worked there, raising her baby and cleaning after travelers. She'd kept to herself and saved every penny.

When the Knepps closed their motel, Julia decided to start fresh. She moved to Charm, rented a ramshackle house that needed some care, and got a job at a fabric and notion store. Days after that, she enrolled Penny in a lovely little Amish school within walking distance.

She'd hoped everything was going to be wonderful. But so far, Julia had met one obstacle after another. Her bills were hard to manage. Taking care of a whole house instead of one tiny motel room was a challenge, too.

She'd get through it, though. She had to. She had no choice but to do anything she could in order to survive.

As she tromped through the snow, she smiled grimly to herself. That, at least, was something she was good at. She'd had a lot of practice surviving. It turned out she would do whatever it took, even lying about her past and taking a new name, if it meant she could take care of Penny.

She was simply going to have to keep doing that. No matter what happened.

As another fierce burst of wind blasted his cheeks, Levi Kinsinger pulled his black knit hat a little lower across his brow.

Stuffing his hands in the pockets of his black coat, he reflected that he shouldn't have worked so late. There was no reason for him to be working past seven at night. Nothing was going on at the lumber mill that couldn't be taken care of tomorrow. He shouldn't have lost track of time.

No, that wasn't true. He'd known it was late. He just hadn't been in any hurry to go back to his house.

And it was definitely a house, not a home.

The fact was, he hated the house he was currently living in. He didn't like its size, the way it was run-down and unkempt, or the fact that strangers had built it.

Furthermore, he didn't like living alone, and he didn't like being within calling distance to the five or six other houses that looked exactly like his own.

Being there was his own fault, of course. When he'd returned home after taking a leave of absence, he'd felt out of sorts. It was probably to be expected. After all, his three siblings had continued their lives while he was still attempting to come to terms with their father's death. While he'd been working construction in the Florida heat, his brother and sisters had moved forward. His older brother, Lukas, had married. So had his sister Rebecca. Now his other sister, Amelia, was practically engaged to Simon Hochstetler.

Yep, all three of his siblings were in various stages of wedded bliss. They were all smiles and full of happy futures. Then, when Lukas and his wife, Darla, announced just before Thanksgiving that they were expecting a baby, Levi felt even more at odds with the rest of them.

He didn't know why, either. He'd prayed for guidance, prayed for understanding, too. But no matter how hard he prayed, he still felt empty inside. So empty that he didn't trust himself to be around his siblings for any length of time. The last thing they needed was for his unhappiness to rub off on them.

Claiming that Lukas and Darla needed to enjoy a little bit of privacy, Levi signed a year lease on a small rental house just south of the mill. Within a week, he'd moved into the drab little place. Though Lukas had asked him several times not to move, Levi's stubbornness had come into play. He'd made his decision and he was going to stand by it, no matter how much he regretted it.

No matter how much he hated the rental with its chipping paint, dirty woodwork, and scarred floors, he knew he'd never tell his siblings that he wasn't happy living in his new place. They didn't need one more thing to worry about.

Actually, he was starting to wonder that same thing. He'd taken to praying to the Lord for guidance. He needed to be the man his father had hoped for him to be, the sooner the better.

All of that was why he was walking home in the cold and in the dark. Because he didn't have any place else to go but work or his house on this dreary little street filled with people who no doubt wished they were living somewhere else, too.

As he walked down Jupiter Street, Levi shook his head. If his father was still alive, he would be shaking his head in shame. Levi needed to get a better attitude. There was not a thing wrong with the houses on Jupiter or the people who lived in them.

Most of the men and women who lived here seemed nice enough. They were hardworking and cordial, if all a bit worn down by life.

It wasn't their fault that their houses and their yards reflected that same attitude. When one worked all the time, trying to make ends meet, one didn't have a lot of time to devote to yard work or painting. Or repair work. It was simply the way it was.

As another gust of wind swept down the street, he braced himself, then increased his pace. At least he'd gone to the grocery store on Saturday and bought a bunch of popcorn, canned soup, and roast beef. He'd make himself a fire and some supper and sit down in his small living room to enjoy it.

Sure, it wasn't going to be the same as one of Amelia's fine meals eaten at the large and well-worn dining room table surrounded by whoever was in the house. But it would do. It would have to—

The direction of his thoughts drew to an abrupt stop when he noticed his neighbor from across the street crawling on her hands and knees near the mailbox.

What in the world?

When he got close, she froze. Though it was dark, he could just make out her panicked features, thanks to a bright moon and one of the neighbors' lit windows. Light-brown eyes. Golden hair. Diamond-shaped face. And the prettiest pair of pale-pink lips he'd ever seen.

Lips that were currently parted as she gaped at him.

Worried, he stopped. "Hey. It's Julia, *jah*?" When she nodded but said nothing, he knelt down to meet her gaze. "What are you doing out here in the dark?"

"Well, to be honest . . . I'm looking for a rock," she replied. As if rock hunting in the dark winter cold was the most natural thing to do in the world.

It was then that he realized she wasn't wearing a coat. Or a sweater. There were also tears in her eyes. And though he'd already known something was wrong, now he knew for sure that something was terribly amiss.

Though he didn't know her hardly at all, he had observed her from time to time. He'd always thought of her as rather calm and peaceful. Never had he seen her acting so flustered. "Any special reason you are needing a rock tonight?" he asked gently.

Leaning back on her haunches, she nodded. "I did something st— I mean silly. I locked myself and Penny out of my house." Her voice thickened with emotion. "I canna find my keys, and I've looked in my purse and pockets at least three times. I need to break a window."

As her words permeated, something happened inside of him. He couldn't bring his father back. He couldn't fit in with his siblings like he wanted to. He wasn't even sure what his future entailed.

But he was a capable man, and he'd worked in a hardware store and lumber mill all of his life. If there was one thing he could do, it was break into a house.

Standing up, he held out his hand for her to take. "I can help you with that."

She stared at him, wide-eyed. "You think so?"

"I know so." Since she hadn't taken his hand yet, he bent toward her a little closer. "Here, let me help you up."

After the briefest hesitation, she tentatively

placed one bared hand in his. It was small and slim. Delicate against his work-roughened palms. "*Danke*," she whispered.

And that was when he realized what had just happened. She believed him. Believed *in* him. Completely.

It was such a positive sensation, so much better than the usual burdens of regrets he'd been carrying around since his father's death. It had been so hard to grieve for a parent all over again. Even harder when he'd realized that just like with his *mamm*, he'd never taken the time to tell his father how much he loved him.

For the first time in weeks, Levi felt like himself again.

"You're welcome," he said, smiling even though she couldn't see his expression. "I'm happy to be of help."

Chapter 2

December 3

Of all the people on her street, Julia couldn't believe that *he* was the person who came to her rescue.

She knew who he was, of course. She'd figured that out by the second week she was in Charm. It seemed everyone knew who Levi Kinsinger was—and they didn't mind gossiping about him, either. Levi was the handsome, headstrong younger son of the wealthiest family in the county. He and his three siblings owned one of the biggest lumber mills in the whole state of Ohio. He was also shrouded by all of the tragedy that the Kinsinger family had incurred over the last decade. First, their mother had died unexpectedly early, leaving their oldest daughter to look after her youngest siblings as best she could while their father grieved and operated the mill. Then, just last year, their father had also been taken to Heaven. He, along with four other workers, had died in a suspicious fire at the mill.

Then there were the other, more lurid stories that were told about him. Whispered stories about

Levi's streak of wildness during his *rumspringa*. His flirting with practically every girl in the county. The way he enjoyed a good joke and never took much very seriously. Those stories had been told with a bit of condemnation mixed with a healthy amount of fondness.

It seemed no one could find it in their hearts to hold Levi Kinsinger to the same standards that everyone else had to aspire to.

At least, that was what the ladies at the sewing shop had said.

From what she had heard, his brother, Lukas, firmly held the reins of the large operation while Levi had once again been impetuously doing whatever he wanted. Folks said that he'd been off running around the country, instead of lightening his brother's load, for the past four months. One customer at work had felt mighty sorry for him, too. She'd said it was normal for him to need some space and time to himself. After all, he needed to come to terms with all that had happened, what with the fire at the mill and the death of his father.

Yes, indeed. It seemed that most folks in Charm were firmly divided on whether a man like Levi had a right to do such a thing or not.

Some thought he was acting like a spoiled man—taking off as soon as his life got difficult, and then forsaking his large, very beautiful house like a child who hadn't gotten his way.

Others had been far more sympathetic.

As for herself, Julia's opinion had rested someplace in the middle. Though she couldn't help but feel more than a little derisive about a person burdening others with responsibilities that he was forsaking, she also realized that there might have been far more going on with him than anyone knew.

She knew from experience that some families had dark secrets and they strived hard to be sure the secrets never saw the light of day.

Besides her big secret, though, her family had been relatively quiet and without the drama her relationship with Luther had been filled with it.

From the time he'd started courting her, he'd excelled at controlling her and using his charm to convince everyone that he was kinder and more forgiving than he was. In private with her, he was a different story. He was demanding and coercive, and not above threatening her in order to keep her doing his will.

Actually, it had only taken one slip for her to understand just how much worse Luther could make her daily life. It was when he thought she had shared with others how he really treated her when no one else was around.

For a time, she'd considered going to her sister for help, but she'd been afraid of what Sarah would say. Sarah hadn't been shy about her misgivings about Luther when they'd first started dating. She'd even called Julia a fool.

How would Sarah have reacted when she'd discovered just how many mistakes Julia had made?

Thinking back to Levi, she figured his reasons for moving out of his grand home were no one's business but his own. *Jah*, it was a dangerous path, judging other people's actions, especially when no one ever really knew what was happening behind someone's closed doors.

There had to be a good, logical reason Levi had moved onto Jupiter Street, just as there had to be a reason that he was a lot more quiet than most everyone said he used to be. Pain and hardship changed a person, even under the best of situations.

Now, as she followed Levi back up the snowy hill that was her front yard, Julia wondered how he planned to open her door. She hadn't missed the fact that he had definitely not picked up any rocks.

After contemplating it for another minute, she gathered her courage and decided to ask. Surely, he wouldn't find fault with such an honest question. "How do you reckon you'll get the door open?"

"I've got something in my pocket that might do the trick," he replied just as he came upon Penny, who was wrapped up in her pile of coats and sweaters. "Hey there," he said in a friendly way. "Aren't you bundled up cute?"

"This is my daughter, Penny," Julia said.

Penny scrambled to her feet. "Hiya," she said uncertainly. "Who are you?"

Before Levi could reply, Julia rushed to reassure her daughter. "This is Mr. Levi Kinsinger, dear. I'm sure you've seen him before. He lives across the street."

"I've seen ya, but *mei mudder* don't ever talk to you."

"I aim to change that," he replied. "I'm hoping we can be friends one day."

While Julia contemplated that idea, Penny gazed at him skeptically. "Did you come over to help us?"

"I did."

After glancing at her mother, Penny gazed up at him. "Did you find a *gut* rock?"

"Not exactly."

Stuffing a hand in his pocket, Levi pulled out a large silver key ring filled with at least twenty keys of all different shapes and sizes. "I've got something in here that usually does the trick," he said as he jingled them softly. "But first, we need to do something else."

Before Julia could ask, Penny stepped closer to him. "What do you need to do?" her daughter asked, staring up at him with wide eyes.

"It ain't me who needs to do something, but your mother," he replied lightly.

"What do you need from me?" Looking at the

contraption in his hand, Julia bit her lip. "I'm afraid I don't know how—"

"Not that," he interrupted. "This." Reaching down, he picked up the black cardigan that was now in a wadded mass and shook it out. "You need to put this on before you catch your death."

Surprised that he did such a thing, she took the sweater from him and slipped it on. Immediately, the soft wool cuddled her skin, feeling almost like a warm hug. "It feels *gut*. Warm."

But instead of looking pleased, he seemed irritated. "You shouldn't have taken it off in the first place. Or your coat."

She knew she'd made a mistake with the front door, but she wasn't about to let him find fault with her parenting skills. Putting a little more heat in her voice, she said, "I didn't have a choice."

"Children need to stay warm, to be sure. But, you should have kept it on. You could get sick. Ain't so?"

Before she could remind him that her health wasn't any of his concern, he jingled the keys in his hand and turned to the door.

"Do you have a key to our *haus*?" Penny asked.

"*Nee*. I'm gonna use this. It's a skeleton key of sorts," he said with a chuckle. "It's come in handy more than I can say over the years."

Penny drew up on her tiptoes to get a better look. "It looks funny, Mr. Kinsinger—"

"You can call me Levi, sugar. No one calls me

Mr. Kinsinger." His smile widened. "I don't think anyone even calls my older *bruder*, Lukas, that. That title was reserved for my dad."

Penny's eyes widened. "Really? Do you call him that?"

"*Nee*. I called him Daed." His voice softened. "And he's not around any longer. He's in Heaven now."

Penny's mouth turned to an O. "My *daed*'s up in there, too."

"That's a real shame."

Penny nodded. "Uh-huh. I don't remember him, though. Do you remember your *daed*?"

"I do." After a brief pause, he cracked a smile. "I also do know that this skeleton key does look strange."

Penny blinked, then giggled. "You're funny, Levi."

"There you go. I'm glad you called me Levi. I like how that sounds."

Even in the dim light, Julia could see that Penny liked that idea, too. However, she most definitely did not. "She'll be calling you Mr. Kinsinger, sir. It's only right."

He looked her way. "Sir, huh?" he asked before he drew his complete attention to the key ring, examining two or three of them in the moonlight before kneeling down on one knee and inserting a long metal key into the slot in the knob.

He joggled it a couple of times, muttered something to himself, then tried a different key. Then the third.

Penny had backed up so that her shoulder blades were resting against Julia's knees. As the minutes passed, Julia reached down and wrapped a cloak more firmly around her body.

She was just about to suggest that she go rock hunting again when Levi wiggled the handle, fussed with the key, and suddenly they all heard a sharp click.

When he turned the handle and opened the door, Penny clapped her hands. "You fixed it!"

"Well, I opened it," Levi clarified. "It wasn't broken. Only locked."

Then, to Julia's disconcertment, he waved a hand. "Let's go inside and get you warm, ladies."

"Now we can have hot chocolate," Penny said. "Right, Mommy?"

"In a minute, Pen."

Penny marched right in, leaving Julia no choice but to follow. When Levi closed the door behind him, her heart lurched as uncertainty took hold of her.

She was also aware of how stark everything probably looked to him. She'd been so intent on saving enough money for rent and her bills, she hadn't been able to buy much. Jared and Connie had given her some old bedroom furniture from the motel, but she had little else.

The walls were bare and the worn Formica

countertops in her kitchen were, too. She also hadn't the time or energy to replace them with anything pretty.

Instead, she had bare windows and a bare wooden floor. And a plain, rather drab-looking brown couch that she'd purchased at a thrift store.

It was a clean room. However, it was also devoid of personality. Lacking warmth.

She feared her house had become a reflection of her soul.

She fidgeted. The polite thing would be to invite him in for something hot to drink, but she wasn't eager to be alone with him, either.

Against the tidy backdrop of her home, he suddenly seemed very big and strong. Almost like he filled up the room, though it might have been his strong, confident personality that did that.

No matter what the reason, as far as she was concerned, Levi was too, well, *everything*.

And she was too aware of all that he was.

But she had to say something. Didn't she? "We haven't lived here very long," she finally stated.

"Me, neither. I just moved in myself."

"I remember the day you moved in." She remembered peeking out the window and noticing that he didn't have too much furniture or belongings. Just like her.

He smiled slightly. "That day feels like ages ago."

She waited for him to tell her more about himself, the way most men liked to do. Or for Levi to ask questions about where they came from and why she was in a small house instead of living with relatives.

But instead, he simply looked on the top of her mantel. "Where are your matches?"

"Hmm?"

"I'm going to light a fire for you, and your stove, too," he said slowly. Looking toward Penny, he smiled. "I bet your hot chocolate is going to taste good now, *jah*?"

Penny nodded. Then, to Julia's additional dismay, Penny scampered to the kitchen, grabbed the ancient tin container that had held long wooden matches from its spot next to the stove, and handed it to Levi.

"*Danke*, Penny. Come with me and we'll get a fire going."

While her five-year-old daughter seemed to have no worries about trusting this man who was a stranger, Julia wasn't of the same mind. "That ain't necessary," she said quickly. "I can get a fire going myself."

Penny drew to a stop and stared hesitantly at Julia.

"Everything is all right, Pen," she said in a rush. "I'm only trying to be a good neighbor. I'm sure Mr. Kinsinger is ready to get on his way."

"Actually, I'm not in that much of a hurry," Levi

said easily. "I'd rather make sure you girls are settled." As if he sensed that Julia was about to protest, he met her gaze. "I'm sure you would agree that a little bit of help never hurts. Ain't so?"

"Of course I appreciate your help. It's mighty kind of you." Not wanting to sound peevish, she tried to pull out the manners her mother had taught her years ago. "If you get a fire going, I'll make hot cocoa for three, and maybe some popcorn, too?" When his eyes widened, she said, "I mean, if you have time?"

Winking at Penny, he said, "I have time for hot chocolate."

"Me, too," Penny said happily.

"Penny, you come in here with me while I make our snacks."

Penny's eyes widened, but she didn't argue. Instead, she followed Julia into the small kitchen and unhooked her cloak and hung it up.

Noticing how chilly it was even inside, Julia dug in a drawer for a flashlight. "Go put on a sweater, Pen. And take off your boots and put on some thick socks. I don't want you to catch a cold."

Without a word, Penny did as she was asked.

Thank goodness for small favors! Julia thought as she pulled out a saucepan for milk and a larger, cast-iron pot for the popcorn.

Though her daughter was only five, she often acted as if she was a grown adult. She had an opinion on just about everything and often shared her thoughts. She wasn't disrespectful, but she often asked a lot of questions.

Julia was glad Penny wasn't in the mood to start peppering Levi with intrusive questions . . . or start telling him about their life when they lived in a motel room.

As far as she was concerned, the less anyone knew about her past, the better.

"She's good at minding you," Levi said.

Startled, she turned to see him leaning just inside the doorway. "I didn't see you there."

"The fire is going good, but I didn't want to sit there by myself. You don't mind if I stand in here with you, do ya?"

"*Nee.*" Realizing that she could have answered him in a friendlier manner, she tried to think of something to talk about. She racked her mind, wondering what she could utter that he would find remotely interesting, but she couldn't seem to think of a single thing.

And because of that, her skin began to heat, no doubt causing giant blotches of red to appear on her cheeks and neck. Oh, how had this day become so, so irritating?

He took a small step back, lengthening the space between them. "I'm sorry. Have I made you uncomfortable?"

"Of course not," she lied. "I just don't know what I should say."

"Really? Funny. I have been thinking the same thing."

"You have?" she blurted before belatedly realizing that she was continually giving him way too much information about herself. Now he knew that she was forgetful, had a chatty daughter, and even though she was a grown woman, she couldn't carry a conversation with a neighbor.

"For sure," he said as if her awkwardness was the most natural thing in the world. "I may be wrong, but I think we're part of the same church district."

"I believe we are."

His brow cleared. "I'm glad I got that right at least. It's too bad that we haven't had an occasion to talk before now."

She added chocolate powder to the milk, pulled out a jar of marshmallows, and then made a show of stirring the mixture. "There's no reason we would have talked. I am a widow and a mother and you are a single man."

"Forgive me, but I think we're both single at the moment. That means we do have something in common."

"Not really, since I'm far older than you."

"Are you really? How do you know that?"

Looking down at the milk mixture, her cheeks burned. "People talk about you."

He blinked, then nodded slowly. "It shouldn't

surprise me, but it still does. So they talk about my age, too?"

"Only in passing." Ack, but this conversation couldn't be any more awkward.

He tilted his head to one side and made a show of examining her closely. "How old are you?"

"I'm thirty."

"I'm twenty-six." A new thread of amusement lit his tone. "I'm no math genius or anything, but I'm thinking that's not that much of an age difference. I sure wouldn't say you were far older than me. Only a couple of years."

She needed to agree. She needed to agree and tell him that she needed him to leave. But her mouth became a traitor. "Four years is a lot when one is young."

"I suppose so," he mused. Just as if what she was saying actually mattered—and it most certainly did not. "I guess it would be quite a big difference if I was ten and you were fourteen."

"Indeed."

"But now, I don't think it matters much, do you?"

"Of course not." After debating a moment or two, she blurted, "The truth is that I have kind of gotten out of the habit of speaking to friends and neighbors." And men. She was really out of practice talking to men her age.

"Maybe you could practice with me."

"You?"

Instead of getting offended, he grinned. "*Jah.* Me. I can be a good friend and neighbor. And though I don't know all the rules about this, I'm fairly sure that friends and neighbors can talk to each other all the time. It doesn't matter what their age."

"I . . . well, yes, I believe you are right about that," she mumbled as the popcorn began to pop, making light pings against the metal lid and sounding almost musical. Oh, but she wished she hadn't locked her key in the house. Then they wouldn't be in the middle of this interminable, awkward conversation!

He studied her another moment before grabbing the heavy pot and shaking it. "Sorry, I can't help myself. Did your mother ever do that?" When she looked as if she didn't follow, he explained. "You know, shake the pot so the kernels didn't burn?"

"I don't remember."

"Hmm. I remember it clear as day." Not facing her, he said, "My *mamm* died years ago."

"I know."

"You know that, too?"

Afraid she'd just admitted that she wasn't near as aloof as she tried to be where he was concerned, she turned off the stove and put both pots off the hot burners. "*Jah.* I work in the notion store and we get a lot of ladies there with time on their hands."

"And?"

"And, well, your family is sometimes a topic of conversation. I couldn't help but hear."

A muscle twitched in his cheek. "You'd think people would have a lot of better things to do besides gossip about me."

"But people weren't being disrespectful," she said quickly. She was treading water in this conversation and was fairly certain she was going down fast. Fumbling around, she continued. "Everyone felt sorry for your family. That's why I remember. I guess I did, too. A young mother dying, leaving four *kinner* and a grieving husband? I'm sure it was very difficult."

"Difficult? *Jah.* It was."

There was nothing more she could say and she felt worse than terrible. Here she was repaying Levi for his help by repeating gossip she'd heard about him. Worse, whenever he saw her in the future, he'd remember that she was clumsy enough to talk about his mother dying after he'd been kind enough to help her inside a locked house.

Inserting a happy lift to her voice, she said, "I'll pour you some hot chocolate now. I think I might even have some whipped cream in the cooler."

But when he looked her way again, his formerly warm expression was guarded. "*Danke*, but I changed my mind."

"I am sorry for mentioning your mother. It was rude. I wasna thinking—"

"It ain't that," he interrupted. "I just remembered I haven't even eaten supper yet. I should probably do that."

"I have some cold cuts. I could make you a sandwich. It's the least I could do for all of your help."

He shook his head slowly. "I didn't do anything special, Julia." After that statement hung in the air another second or two, he slapped a hand against his thigh. "Well, it's been a long day. I worked late and lost track of time. I should go on home. Tell Penny goodbye for me, would you?"

He was already backing out of her kitchen. "Oh. Yes, of course I'll do that." Hurriedly following him, she said, "*Danke* for your help with the lock."

"I'm glad I was nearby. Next time you lock yourself out in the winter, don't take off your coat and sweater, okay?"

He surely thought she was both rude and a fool. "I don't plan for there to be a next time."

"Lots of things happen that we don't plan for, Julia."

"That is true," she muttered to herself as she watched him walk quietly out of the kitchen, then heard him open the front door and leave.

Feeling at a loss, she wondered if she had been

so rude or was he simply extremely sensitive about his mother. Did the loss still fill him with so much pain that he couldn't talk about her?

Or was it her gossiping?

Or, she wondered, as she carefully poured some hot chocolate into a mug, was it something else? Had he felt the same tension between them that she did?

She supposed it didn't really matter.

Actually, none of what they'd shared had meant all that much. Well, nothing except for the last part . . . that a lot of things happened that couldn't be planned for.

That statement had never felt more true.

Chapter 3

❄ ❄ ❄

December 4

"I'd say you were trying to shame us all by trying to make a wonderful-*gut* impression on your boss, but you own the place," Simon Hochstetler said to Levi as he poured himself another cup of coffee in the small break room in the back of Warehouse Seven.

"Good impression?" Levi tried to smile around his yawn. He really was tired, the result of staying up far too late in his empty house and thinking about his new neighbor, her little girl, and why he'd reacted the way he did to their conversation about his mother's death.

"You know what I mean," Simon said. "I heard you were the last one here last night and the first to arrive."

Simon had been a good friend for most of Levi's life. Now he was about to be his brother-in-law, thanks to Amelia claiming him like he was a prized goose. But their close relationship didn't mean there was any reason to let down his guard. If he did, there was a good chance he'd start to share too much about how hard of a time he was having with the fact that both of his parents were now gone. Though he had his siblings, he was feeling a little lost. He was a grown man and far too old to be dwelling on the fact that he missed having his parents around or that he should have told each of his parents how much he'd loved them before their deaths.

Because he still hadn't dealt with it, he was feeling close to breaking.

"I might have been the first to arrive or I might not have. It doesn't really matter."

"Considering that I'm one of the managers, I think it does. Is something going on I'm not aware of?"

Simon's voice held a note of concern in it, making Levi realize that his good friend was genuinely trying to help him. "Not at all," he said lightly. "I just want to do my part, that's all."

"Doing your part doesn't mean making the rest of us look bad," Roman joked as he joined them, a thick custard-filled donut in his hand. Roman was a bear of a man blessed with a loving wife who made sure he always had a donut for his morning break.

"Seems to me you should be thinking about your heart and waist, Roman," Levi said. "That donut diet ain't healthy for a man of your age."

"I'm forty-two, not sixty-two." Puffing up his chest, Roman deepened his voice. "I'm also, I might add, in fine form. My *frau* told me so last night."

"Thanks for sharing that," Simon teased.

"Anytime," he said smugly. "Besides, her opinion is all I care about . . . just like you only seem to have ears for the beautiful Amelia, Simon."

To Levi's amusement, Simon didn't bother to deny Roman's statement. "Amelia is beautiful, that is true. And I do only care about her feelings about my physique. Just for the record, she finds me attractive. Mighty attractive."

"Tattoos and all?"

Simon winked. "For sure and for certain."

As a couple of the men around them laughed, Levi started to feel like his collar was fastened too tight. "That's my sister, man. Don't talk about her like that."

Immediately, Simon turned serious. "Don't find fault where there is none to find. I would never disrespect Amelia. You know that."

Levi turned back to the coffee maker and

topped off his cup. He needed to get a grip on himself and do it quickly, too. Simon was exactly right. He hadn't done a thing to warrant that warning from Levi. Actually, there was likely no one in the world who thought as highly of Amelia as Simon.

"You're right. I apologize. I guess my temper is short. I didn't get a lot of sleep last night."

Simon crossed his arms over his chest. "Going back to what you said earlier . . . is there a problem going on that we're not aware of?"

"*Nee.* Everything is running like clockwork. Profits are up, too."

"That's *gut* news," Roman announced.

Levi smiled at Roman, then made himself meet the eyes of the six or seven other men who were congregating around the coffee maker. "It is *gut* news, indeed. I haven't spoken to Lukas about the details yet, but I'm certain Kinsinger's will be paying out some Christmas bonuses this year."

As he'd hoped, all of the men looked pleased by the statement. After a few minutes passed, each got his coffee and turned away, leaving Levi alone with Simon and Roman once again.

Simon grinned. "Thank you for that, Levi. I've been trying to find a way to inspire my team."

"What do they need inspiration for?"

"Sam Buckley is driving the semi today, and you know how he is. He's either going to be complaining about the roads, his work, or my men."

"And Sam's load is either going to be perfect . . . or perfectly ruined," Roman finished.

Levi whistled low. "I'll hope for the former and pray for the latter."

"*Danke.*"

"You still seem awfully chipper for a man about to deal with Buckley," Roman said. "At the risk of irritating Levi again, is it all Amelia's doing?"

"Not this time." Smiling broadly, he said, "I'm happy because my sister, Tess, has officially opened The Refuge. She stopped by the house this morning to tell me that three teenagers stopped by last night and played Ping-Pong for hours."

"The Refuge, huh? I like that name."

"I do, too," Simon said. "Tess said everyone needed a safe place in their lives."

"I'm glad it opened. It's going to be a blessing for many in the area." Levi smiled. Tess had seen a need in the community for teenagers to congregate. A safe place where they could have fun and not get into trouble . . . and find some adults who would listen to any problems that they might be experiencing.

It was exactly the type of place where Tess, Simon, and their brother, Jeremy, would have given just about anything to have when they were growing up in an abusive home.

"It is a blessing, to be sure. But it's also the result of a lot of hard work. Tess has been talking with ministers of every church in the area, hoping to gain their support. Finally, it's paying off."

"I'm happy for you."

"*Danke.*"

"Do you need any more shelves built? If so, I'd be happy to help out," Levi asked.

"I'll ask, but I think Tess is now hoping for more tables and chairs. She's even hoping to make one of the back rooms a sleeping area."

"I can make chairs for you," Roman offered.

"*Danke*, but I don't think your handcrafted chairs are what we have in mind. We're looking for something more serviceable."

Roman looked mildly affronted. "What is that supposed to mean?"

"You make works of art," Simon countered. "If we need anything built, it needs to be sturdy and simple. The furniture needs to be tough enough to withstand abuse from dozens of teenagers, or even any small children who visit with their mothers."

"I can make furniture like that, too."

"Most of us working here can as well. I don't want to waste your talents by having you make serviceable furniture."

"It ain't a waste if it's being used. Ain't so?"

"You're right," Simon replied. "*Danke.*"

As Roman's thoughtful statement rang in his mind, a new idea came to Levi. Feeling energized, he pointed to the bulletin board. "You know that the men here are always looking for a way to help out in the community, especially around the holidays. I bet I could get a work group together."

Sipping his coffee, Roman nodded. "That would be the best way to get things done quickly. Many hands do make quick work."

"It's settled, then," Levi said. "I'll write up something and pin it up tomorrow. Before you know it, we'll all be at The Refuge, building furniture for teenagers to treat roughly."

Simon slapped him on the back. "Thanks, brother. I'd appreciate that. Tess will, too."

Levi was tempted to give him grief about calling him brother, but he didn't have the will to do that. It simply sounded too good.

Chapter 4

❄ ❄ ❄

December 5

Every once in a while, Tess Hochstetler took time to give thanks for the Lord's guidance. She'd received so many blessings over the last year, many which she considered to be answers to prayers.

How else could she explain that she'd reunited with both her brothers, had quit her busy job as a pharmaceutical rep, and now was doing a job that was about a hundred times more meaningful, and it was back in the same town where she grew up?

God had been so good.

Jill, her adoptive mother, also played a large role in the recent changes in her life. Years ago, when Tess had been just a teenager and was living on the streets, Jill had reconfigured her whole life in order to help her.

Over time, Jill had become Tess's good friend and advisor. She'd also continued to help people in need whenever she could.

Now Tess was excited about the idea of paying it forward.

What made it even better was that Tess could work at her new job in complete comfort, too.

At the moment her hair was in a ponytail. She didn't have on a bit of makeup, and she was wearing an old stretched-out turtleneck and an even older pair of jeans. She felt comfortable, relaxed, and at ease.

Which was good, considering The Refuge was small, rundown, didn't have enough furniture in it, and could use a good dose of air freshener. Yep, she absolutely had her work cut out for her. But that was okay.

Every time Tess Hochstetler looked around the building, she felt an enormous sense of pride. Little by little, she was taking something that had been abandoned and making it useful . . . just like she hoped the kids would feel about themselves.

Looking at her jeans, worn sweater, and warm fuzzy boots, she had to smile to herself. This place—and the kids in need—were a lot like she used to be.

Back when she'd been growing up here in Charm, she'd been sure she and her two brothers had been forgotten. She'd been raised Amish in a small farmhouse on the outskirts of the area. And though the Amish by nature were kind-natured, faithful people, her father had not been. She and her siblings had endured years of abuse and neglect before each of them had left.

She'd run away barely a year after her older

brother, Jeremy, with only a couple of dollars to her name. Fear of the unknown and being hungry had been nothing compared to the fear she'd felt on a daily basis in her own house.

But what living in those circumstances had done was make her so desperate for a way out that she'd abandoned her little brother. She'd left Simon to bear the consequences of her actions.

And he certainly had borne the brunt of that.

Now, though they'd spent more than a decade apart, they were forging a new bond. At first, it had been tenuous, but now it was obvious that they still had some things in common, even though Simon was still Amish and she had adopted an English lifestyle.

Taking out a notebook from her backpack, she grabbed one of her few chairs and got to work. There were so many people she needed to contact—from tutors to ministers to college students eager to earn volunteer credit—she could only take care of things in small batches. Otherwise, it became too overwhelming.

Just as she pulled out her cell phone, a brief knock sounded at her door. Before she could rise, the door opened a few inches.

Alarmed, she jumped to her feet and hurried over to meet the visitor.

"Yes?" she asked. "May I help you?"

To her surprise, it wasn't another teen but a police officer in full uniform. He was tall, broad shouldered, and looked like he could bench press two hundred pounds.

He also happened to look as surprised to see her as she was to see him.

"Hi. Are you the owner of this place?"

She drew herself up to her full, unimpressive height of five foot five. "I am."

He held out a hand. "I'm Officer Perry. I heard a little about this place from a friend of mine who's a social worker." Looking just beyond her, he added, "I thought I should check it out."

Ignoring his hand, she went on guard. "Why?" she asked quickly, her voice slightly higher than normal. "Is there a problem?" Only after the fact did she realize how argumentative she sounded. Though she didn't really care for the police—with the exception of Jill, her foster mother—Tess had long come to terms with the fact that it was better to get along with them than not. "I'm sorry. I didn't mean how that sounded."

He looked at her more closely. "How did it sound to you?"

"Like I was picking a fight." Ack. Of course, now she was coming across even worse.

But instead of looking irritated, he merely laughed and held out a business card. "I should have introduced myself better. I'm a cop, of course. But my job is mainly to work with the local schools. I visit all of the kids from first grade to grade twelve."

"The schools here are that dangerous?"

Amusement lit his eyes. "Not at all. I talk to them about making good choices, stranger danger, drugs . . ." He paused. "And abuse."

It seemed God had brought this man into her life when she most needed him. He'd given her a chance to work with someone who could actually help children who were at risk. She needed to get over her aversion to policemen, relax, and ask for his help.

At last, she claimed the card and scanned it. "I'm Tess Hochstetler. Won't you come sit down in one of my three chairs?"

As she'd hoped, he laughed. "Thanks. That would be great."

Together, they walked back to where she'd been sitting. She returned to her chair, and he took the one across from her. Though he was in his uniform, he managed to look comfortable and at ease. She wondered if it was from practice or if he actually did find his polyester uniform, complete with gun, shield, and radio comfortable.

He also didn't seem bothered by the way she was examining him. Instead, he folded his hands loosely between his knees and gave her his full attention. "Tell me about yourself and this place."

"I'm hoping it will be a safe haven for teens. I'm calling it The Refuge."

"That's what I heard. I like the sign out front, too."

"Thanks. My brother made it." Simon had designed and built a good-sized sign at the mill and had even stained it a dark walnut color. She thought it was understated and eye-catching at the same time.

Feeling marginally more at ease, she continued. "In a nutshell, I grew up here in Charm. Things weren't good at my house. When I couldn't take it anymore, I ran away and ended up on the streets. I'm hoping to prevent other kids from having to go to the lengths I did to feel safe."

"So you started The Refuge."

She nodded. "Yes. I had wanted to think of something a little catchier, but the name seemed to fit, I think. I wanted a comforting sounding name to the place, for scared teens or women to know that it would be a safe place."

"That's commendable. I hope it works out." But his expression was doubtful. "You might get some kids to trust you, but there's also a good possibility that you might not. As you know, we've got a large Amish population, and they can be a little wary about reaching out to English organizations."

"I grew up Amish. My younger brother joined the faith and lives locally."

He blinked. "Really? Wow. You surprised me."

"Why is that?" she blurted. Belatedly remembering her personal vow to try to get along with him better, she began again. "I mean, lots of people in the area who grow up Amish decide not to be baptized."

"That's true. But most of the time, I can hear the accent. You sound like a city girl, through and through."

"I guess I am now. I've been living in the suburbs of Columbus for most of the last fifteen years."

"That explains it, then."

"What about you?"

"I grew up over in New Philly." He rolled his eyes. "Back in the day, we thought we were city folk ourselves."

She laughed. "It's all perspective, I guess."

"So, are you planning to stay around here for a while?" He smiled, his expression warm and inviting. And for the first time since he'd arrived, she actually looked at him. He had dark hair, almost black. And dark-brown eyes, too. Olive skin and a well-defined square jaw.

"I am," she said, kind of surprising herself even as she said the words. "I want to be near my brothers." Especially Jeremy, whom she was just getting to know again.

"I'm glad to hear that."

Her stomach fluttered. Was he worried about her place . . . or thinking about her? "Any special reason why you'd say that?"

"Not really . . . except that I want to know how I'll be able to see you again."

All the anxiety that had disappeared returned in a flash. "Why would you want to do that? Do you expect trouble, Officer Perry?"

"Not at all."

She didn't do well with his word games. "I'm sorry, but you're going to have to explain things a little more clearly for me."

"Tess, I'm trying to tell you—very awkwardly, obviously—that I want to get to know you better."

"Because of my past?"

He laughed. "Because there's something about you that makes me smile. I'm hoping we could maybe be friends?"

"Oh."

He studied her closely. "Oh? Does that mean you'd rather not be friends?"

He sounded almost disappointed. Feeling bad, she said, "I'm not trying to be difficult . . ." Her voice drifted off then, because, what could she say? She didn't have a lot of experience with men who simply wanted to be her friend. She also had next to no experience being friends with men who were cops.

He waited a couple of beats for her to continue. When she didn't, he nodded. "Okay. I understand." He took a breath. "I don't expect that you'll have any trouble, Tess. I hope not. But if something happens that worries you, don't forget about my card, okay?" he asked as he stood up and started walking toward the door. “And by the way, my first name is Ken. I’d appreciate it if you called me that.”

Momentarily speechless, she nodded.

A warm glow returned to his gaze. “It was real nice meeting you, Tess.”

“Yeah. I mean, it was nice to meet you, too. Ken.”

He grinned again, then closed the door behind him.

Staring at the closed door, Tess blinked. If she wasn’t mistaken, a police officer had just been flirting with her. She surely hadn’t seen that coming.

Now all she had to do was figure out how to deal with it and what she was going to do if he came back.

Chapter 5

❄ ❄ ❄

December 5

"It's almost four o'clock, Julia," Angel Beck said from her stool at the back of the Fabric and Notion Shop. "You ought to pack up and get on your way. You don't want to be late for your daughter's party."

Looking up from the quilt she was sewing, Julia gaped at her boss. "It's that time already? Where did the day go?"

"Where it always does. It flew by too quickly." Walking over to Julia, Angel had to stop a couple of times to catch her breath.

Poor Angel was in her seventies and had recently been experiencing some pain in her joints. Every time Julia had tried to encourage Angel to stay home and rest, the lady had brushed off her advice, saying that a little bit of aches and pains was not going to get the best of her.

Julia admired the lady's gumption, but she was really starting to worry about her. "Are you sure you're going to be all right here by yourself until it's time to close? I could maybe call Hope to come in for a spell."

"You'll do no such thing. I have a hard time walking, that's true. But I'm going to settle myself behind the register and let the customers come to me."

"And they will." Everyone loved Angel and went out of their way to help her in the shop. "Now, who is going to walk you home?"

"One of my grandsons. Two of 'em work at Kinsinger's, you know. This store is right on their way home." Before Julia could say more, she made a shooing sign with her hands. "Don't you worry about me."

"How can I not worry when you do so much for me?"

"You are right. We have a good partnership, don't we?" Angel asked, her eyes warming.

"That we do. I'm so thankful for you."

Angel scoffed. "Don't you be getting emotional on me, girl. You walking in here and asking for a job was an answer to my prayers. Though I hate the fact that you and Penny are alone in the world, I'm mighty glad you came into my life."

Angel's words were so sweet, Julia was tempted to confess that she and her daughter weren't exactly alone in the world. She had parents, she just didn't communicate with them.

And Penny had a father, she just didn't know he was alive.

No one did.

"Julia? Are you all right, dear?"

"Oh! *Jah.* Of course." She smiled tightly. In spite of herself, Julia felt a lump form in her throat. Angel was a welcome reminder of how good most people can be. Just like Connie and Jared, the kind couple who had hired her on a whim at the motel.

No matter how hard she tried, Julia knew that her first instinct was to not trust anyone. Luther had effectively taught her that—and had shown her time and again the consequences of relying on other people.

When was she going to be able to realize that Luther was just one person? Yes, he'd been important to her and was Penny's father. But he wasn't everything to her anymore, and more importantly, he was nothing to Penny.

Holding a hand out for Julia's apron, Angel said, "Now, missy, I've answered just about all the questions that I aim to. Go on before your sweet girl misses her party."

Finally satisfied that everything was going to be all right, Julia handed over the apron, carefully folded the Christmas baby quilt that she'd been working on, and slipped on her cloak.

"I'll be in tomorrow afternoon, Angel."

"Oh, I'm glad you mentioned that. I almost forgot to tell ya that Hope is going to be working tomorrow." Smiling sweetly, she said, "She needed some extra hours and I figured you'd enjoy the chance to spend more time with Penny."

She was looking at her so expectantly, Julia made herself look as agreeable as she could. "I . . . *jah*, I always enjoy having more time for Penny."

"That's just what I told Hope! You enjoy your day off now."

"Oh. *Jah*. Well, you, too." She smiled weakly, then dashed out the door.

Only when she was walking home by herself did she acknowledge her disappointment. She *was* disappointed. She'd been counting on those hours to pay her bills. She'd also needed the time at the store to work on her quilt so she could sell it before Christmas. Penny had her heart set on a "real" baby doll, one like the Englishers played with—one with eyes and a mouth and cute outfits to dress her in.

And because Penny asked for so little, Julia hated to disappoint her.

But what Penny didn't know—and what Julia hoped she would never find out—was that their financial situation wasn't the best. Actually, they were struggling. There was precious little money for extras, let alone expensive dolls.

As she continued the ten-minute walk from the store to her house, she mentally maneuvered around her financial situation. If she took the quilt home and stayed up late a couple of nights in a row perhaps she could get it done within the week.

Working at home would be tricky, of course.

She didn't have a quilt frame. She'd also have to rely on the natural light from the windows in order to stitch. Work would be a lot slower.

But it could be done.

Slowly, she smiled. There was the right attitude! With the Lord's help and prayer, she could do it. She knew she could. She would just have to hope and pray that someone would want to buy the quilt right away, and for full price. Then, she could put the doll on layaway.

She could even admit to Angel that she would like to work more hours, too.

If she did all of that . . . why, there was a fair chance that she'd be able to give Penny her doll on Christmas Day.

"*Danke*, *Got*," she whispered. "Just when I was feeling hopeless you reminded me that there's always a will and a way."

"Julia, either you are intent on solving all the world's problems or you have some mighty big ones of your own," a voice called out from behind her. "I sure hope it's not the latter."

Startled, she looked behind her, then wanted to cover her face with her hands. Here she was, talking to herself in broad daylight. "Was I talking to myself again?"

Levi came up to her side. She noticed that today he had on a Kinsinger Lumber hoodie over a plain white shirt, and thick dark wool trousers. She couldn't deny that the dark-gray sweatshirt with the forest-green emblem brought out his golden blond hair and brown eyes.

Those eyes, brown like hers, yet flecked with blue and gold, now sparkled in amusement. "I'm not sure if you were or you weren't. I just happened to hear you mumbling under your breath. At least, I think that's what you were doing."

"I might have been." Deciding she might as well laugh it off, she added, "It's a poor habit, I'm afraid."

"There are worse ones."

She couldn't argue with that. "I suppose there are." Not sure how to move on from that, she increased her pace. It really was time to get back home.

He smiled at her again, seemed to consider saying something, but then merely looked forward again.

"Was there something you wanted to tell me, Levi?" she asked.

"There was, but I don't want to be rude." Before she could comment on that, he blurted, "It's just that, well, I wasn't lying when I said that you looked worried. Are you okay?"

"*Jah.* I was just thinking about some things." Not wanting to sound so vague, she smiled. "Christmas."

His expression eased. "Ah, yes. Christmas. Are you thinking about all the baking you've got to do? That seems to be all my sisters ever talk about."

"Baking and gifts."

"Don't worry, I'm sure you'll get it all done. Amelia and Becky always do . . . even when they say they have too much to do."

"I'm sure things will happen the way they need to happen."

"That's the attitude." After they'd gone a few more feet, he said, "Are you headed home now, too?"

"Too? Isn't it a bit early for you to be leaving work?" Realizing it might sound as if she'd been paying far too much attention to his comings and goings, she quickly added, "I mean, it seems kind of early for you."

He frowned. "It is, but I had a good reason."

"What is that?"

"I've got to clean my house. My siblings are coming over a couple of evenings from now."

She was surprised by how beleaguered he sounded. He'd given her every indication that he was close to his brother and sisters. Why, his tone when he'd mentioned Amelia and Rebecca had been filled with love. "You don't like them to visit you?"

"Not especially."

"Really? I was under the impression that you were close with your siblings."

"Oh, I am. I would just rather go back to my

family's home instead of entertaining them at my place."

"Can't you tell them that?"

"Not this time. They want to come over again." He grimaced. "Last time they visited, it didn't turn out too well."

"I'm sure this visit will go fine."

"I don't know about that. They are going to be filled with criticisms, you mark my words. I can already hear how ugly they are going to think my place is." With a groan he added, "What is worse is that I'm likely going to be hearing their opinions for weeks. *Nee*, likely for the rest of my life."

Though she knew he hadn't meant it to come off like it did, it sounded rather harsh. "I'm sure they'll be nicer than that," she chided. Then, thinking that he was pretty much telling her that he was embarrassed about where he lived—where she lived, too, right across the street from him—she added, "You know, these houses aren't that bad. There are worse places to live."

"You are right. But what I'm trying to say is that even if my house was brand-new and shiny, they wouldn't think much of it."

"Because?"

"Because they don't understand why I'm living here at all."

Put that way, Julia admitted that she didn't understand it herself. The homes on their street were small and unassuming. They were nothing to be ashamed of, of course, but they certainly were far from the large house on the hill that was the Kinsinger homestead.

She was tempted to ask Levi why he was living on Jupiter Street in the first place. But since that seemed rather intrusive, she concentrated on his problem.

Though she didn't have any experience about welcoming wealthy relatives into a modest home, he looked so uneasy she gave it her best shot. "All you have to do is light a fire and offer them something warm to drink. They'll feel cozy and right at home, I bet."

"I'll have to settle for it not looking too dirty," he said. "Right now, I'll be grateful if my sister Amelia doesn't notice how bad my kitchen floor looks." He shook his head. "I don't know how I'm ever going to get it clean."

"Do you have a decent mop?" So many people never invested in a good mop.

"Ah, *nee*." Eyes sparkling with amusement, he added, "I don't have even a bad one."

"There's your first problem, Levi. In order to clean well, you need the proper tools. Would you like to borrow mine?" They were almost home now. Stopping at the foot of her driveway, she saw that Mrs. Crane, her babysitter, was already home with Penny. "It will be no trouble for me to run inside to get it for you."

He stopped, seeming to consider it. Then he spoke. “Do you have a moment to see what I’m talking about?”

She really didn’t, but there was something in his eyes that told her that he needed her to know more about himself. Almost like he needed her to be his friend. That idea was so tempting, she nodded. “I need to get home to Penny, but I can spare five minutes or so.”

He grinned. Obviously delighted. “That’s all the time you’re gonna need. Once you actually see what I’m up against, I think you’ll understand why I’m in such a panic. Come on.”

Intrigued, she followed him across the street. When they walked inside his front door, the scene that met her eyes was so, so . . . appalling, she had to remind herself several times not to laugh.

Dust bunnies were in every corner. Old furniture that looked like he’d picked it off the curb waited for them in the living room. Each piece was placed against the walls like they were afraid to venture any farther into the house than they had to.

Walking past Levi, she stepped into the kitchen, then was tempted to turn right back around. Grime lay thick on every surface. And that stove? Ack! She would be afraid to turn it on.

He stood silently while watching her inspect the two rooms. Now a worry line was on his forehead. “I guess it looks pretty bad, huh?”

If she knew him better, she would ask him if he was attempting a joke. Though she didn't want to hurt his feelings, there was nothing she could say to ease the truth. "It looks worse than bad. It looks, I'm sorry to say, rather unhealthy."

His tawny eyebrows raised. "Unhealthy?"

"To be sure." Pointing to the range top with its caked-on dirt and grease, she wrinkled her nose. "I don't think anything that comes from this stove can be edible."

He rubbed the back of his neck. "I haven't cooked a meal for myself on it yet."

"Levi, you're going to need more than a mop to set things right. You're going to need some powerful cleaners and a whole lot of time."

Looking even more dejected, he said, "I don't have either of those." He grunted. "Maybe I can tell Lukas and my sisters to stay away a little longer." He swallowed. "Like indefinitely."

"Cleaning this place will take a lot of work, but it's possible. You seem fairly capable, too. Just take it one room at a time."

"Good advice."

Though Julia knew she had to get home to Penny, she couldn't resist asking him something. "I'm feeling pretty confused. You seem so competent. How is it that you've let this place get so bad? A lot could be improved if you took the time to do a little mopping and dusting now and then."

"I don't really know where to start. It wasn't clean when I rented it."

"You didn't notice that it was really dirty?"

"I guess I didn't really care." He paused, looking like he was about to tell her more, then stopped himself just in time.

She was beginning to understand that there was more bothering him about his siblings' visit than a dirty oven and floor. "Do you care now?"

"*Jah.* I care now. I am capable in a lot of ways. I can manage groups of men. I can clean out horse stalls. But I don't like housework, especially for this house. I've been avoiding it by working at the mill all the time."

His honesty made her realize how nosy she had sounded. "I'm sorry. My tongue is getting the best of me. I shouldn't have sounded so rude."

"If I didn't want to tell you, I wouldn't have. I don't always like talking about myself, but I don't lie."

"I don't like talking about myself, either," she admitted.

"The reason I brought you over here is to show you what I have to tackle. Fact is, I need a housekeeper. I stink at cleaning. I don't have the patience for it."

Just as she was about to nod in agreement, she realized that the Lord had just given her a way to ease her financial situation. "Do you have a housekeeper in mind to hire?"

"No. Do you know of anyone? I'll pay well. Someone who wants a lot of work right away?"

"As a matter of fact, I do."

"Would you give me her name?" he asked eagerly. "If you can think of a woman who wouldn't look at this place and turn right around screaming, I'll be grateful."

"I do know someone, and so far she hasn't screamed yet."

"Are you talking about yourself?"

"Yep. I'll be glad to help you clean your place up."

"This wasn't why I brought you over. You don't have to do this."

"I really would like to help. I need the money for some Christmas presents for Penny, you see." Lifting her chin, she said, "She wants a baby doll. Not a fabric one, but a real one, like you see on the department store shelves. I aim to get it for her."

Understanding filled his expression. "Are you free tomorrow?"

"I am. My boss at the fabric store didn't need me so I can come over as soon as Penny goes to school, around eight in the morning."

"I'll wait for you here and we'll discuss everything then. Sound all right?"

"It sounds very all right. I should go now."

He walked her to the door. "Thank you, Julia. You are going to be an answer to my prayers."

He'd been an answer to her prayers, too.

After smiling at him, she headed back home. Already her shoulders felt as if a hundred pounds had been lifted off of them.

When she walked through the door, Penny ran to her side. "Mommy, you're late," she chided. "I thought I was going to miss my party."

"I had to talk to our neighbor across the way, but now I'm here, child. And we have plenty of time to make it to your friend's *haus*. Go wash your face."

While Penny did as she was bid, Julia paid Mrs. Crane. "*Danke* for watching her today."

"It was no trouble." Gesturing toward the kitchen, she said, "We were able to make some peanut butter cookies for Penny to take to the party."

Lightly browned and puffy, they were half-dollar-sized and had the distinctive crisscrosses on the top, along with what looked like chocolate sprinkles. "They look wonderful-*gut* and smell heavenly."

"They taste good, too," Mrs. Crane said with a smile.

Unable to help herself, Julia picked up one that was still warm from the oven and bit into the doughy goodness. The taste of sweet peanut butter filled her mouth. "They are delicious."

Mrs. Crane laughed. "I'm glad you are giving one a try. You need to treat yourself more often."

She snapped her fingers. “I almost forgot to ask something. Are you going home for Christmas break?”

“*Nee.* This is my home.”

“I meant with your family.” Mrs. Crane eyed her closely. “Where did you say you were from again?”

Julia knew she hadn’t said. It was second nature to keep everything about her past as hidden as possible. “Just a tiny town a few hours from here.”

Mrs. Crane smiled, obviously waiting for Julia to finally share something more about herself. When Julia only took another bite of her cookie, she slipped on her coat. “Well, dear. Let me know when you need me again. You know I always have time for Penny.”

“*Danke.*”

Julia opened the door for her, then stood next to it as she watched her neighbor carefully navigate her way down the sidewalk. It had been shoveled, but sometimes there were slippery spots that an elderly lady might slip on.

Once she was satisfied that Mrs. Crane had made it back to her home four doors down, she closed the door and went about arranging the cookies in a plastic container for the party.

You need to treat yourself more often.

Had her life come to that? Taking a single cookie counted as allowing herself to have a treat? That was a little disturbing.

Not because a cookie wasn't a treat. But because it felt as if it had become a metaphor for what her life had become. Her relationship with Luther had been painful. Often it was filled with hurt and shame. She'd hated that she'd trusted a man who had ended up belittling and abusing her.

But even more, she'd been ashamed that she'd become engaged to him. Sometimes, in the middle of the night, she even allowed herself to accept the awful truth. She might have even married him if she hadn't become pregnant. For some reason, she'd begun to think that she hadn't mattered all that much.

She'd put up with so much from him, and kept it all secret from her parents.

She'd only left when she'd feared his abuse could hurt her unborn baby. And instead of holding her head up and telling others about how mean and controlling he'd been, she'd simply run away.

Hating those memories, hating how weak she'd been, Julia forced herself to return to the present.

Now, she had bills to pay and a job to keep. Now, she had a daughter to raise and suppers to cook. Then there was laundry and cleaning.

Somehow, along the way, she'd forgotten that she was important, too. Glad she had no mirror in the house, she could only imagine how awful she looked.

No wonder that Levi Kinsinger had been so

kind to her and accepted her working for him. Instead, he probably felt like Angel and Mrs. Crane did. That someone needed to give her a helping hand.

"Mommy, we need to go!" Penny called out impatiently. She was already standing in front of the door, her feet snug in her favorite red snow boots.

Picking up the plastic container of cookies, Julia smiled at her daughter. "Then I think we had better get on our cloaks and boots and mittens and start walking."

As expected, Penny raced to the door to put on her cloak and boots. "Momma, this time we need to remember the key."

"You are right, child. I need to remember that today as well."

Things were looking up. She was settled in her own neat-as-a-pin house. She had a good job at the notion store and another part-time one to help pay for extras. She also had a friend in Levi.

This was going to be the best December in years.

Chapter 6

❄❄❄

December 6

December was Luther Schrock's least favorite month of the year.

While walking to his workplace at the Middlefield general store, he wondered if he'd ever grow to enjoy the month.

He fairly doubted it.

December held nothing but bitter and hurtful memories for him. It was the month Mary, his wife, had died in childbirth. She'd contracted some infection while pregnant and the birthing process had aggravated it. That weakness not only cost him his wife but their son.

His son.

How could a man ever come to terms with that? He didn't think it would ever be possible.

To make matters worse, he now knew that December was the month of his daughter's birthday.

The daughter he'd never seen.

The daughter who didn't even know he existed.

Every time he thought about Julia Brubacher and her betrayal, he was tempted to ram his fist through a wall. The woman's rejection of all that they'd been together seemed to have no bounds. So much so, Luther found he was still having a difficult time processing that one woman could do so much damage to his heart and soul.

Julia had been his first love. He courted her in earnest and had hardly been able to see anything but her. Actually, he'd been so smitten, so anxious to be around her all the time, he hardly allowed her to be away from his side for more than a couple of hours at a time.

Now that time had passed, he realized his infatuation didn't make a lot of sense. There really wasn't anything special about her. Not really. She wasn't even particularly pretty. Oh, she had pleasing brown eyes that were rather round. And a dimple in her full cheeks that was always rather pink. There was a sweet innocence surrounding her that had been hard for him to ignore. In addition, her outlook on life had been open and full of wonder. He, with his dark thoughts and cynicism, found her hope and innocence to be addictive. He hadn't been able to get enough of that sweetness.

Now, he realized, her sweetness had only been an act. It was covering up a spiteful, secretive heart. He should have known better. He should have been smarter and realized she couldn't be trusted.

He should have never been so taken in by her lies and subterfuge.

She was young and eager when he started courting her. At first, she was easy to control. Easy to bend to his will. But then, she became more difficult to manage. He'd been forced to remind her who was in charge of their relationship, who would always be in charge.

For a time, Julia was biddable. She minded him better, seemed to understand and appreciate his desire to take care of her. So much so that she hadn't protested too much when he'd taken her to bed. She seemed to understand as much as he did that they needed to rush the physical aspect of their relationship.

He'd been sure she understood why. He wanted her. But he'd also felt the need to ensure that she wouldn't even think of straying. He'd had to make it so she would be ruined for anyone else.

But then, weeks later, she pushed him again—when she talked to another man after church. He was forced to make his displeasure known. After, she tried to break things off with him.

He'd only laughed at her naiveté. "You could be with child, Julia. You could be carrying *my* child," he reminded her.

When she shook her head and protested that it didn't matter, he shook her hard. Then, when she was on the ground, he stated things clearly yet again. "You can't ever leave me, Julia. I will never allow it. You are mine. You will always be mine. Always. Do you understand?"

Looking pained, Julia nodded at last. Tears of regret streamed down her face. She apologized for angering him. Promised that she would try to be smarter in the future.

He dropped her home that evening, sure that she had learned her lesson.

But the next day when he came to call, her parents informed him that she'd taken off the night before. Without a note. Without any indication about where she was going.

She'd simply left.

First, he'd been angry but hopeful. He was sure that she was going to come to her senses and return home. He was prepared to listen to her apology and forgive her—*after* she'd admit that she was very blessed to have him and would promise to never disobey him again.

But then, when she didn't show up after two days, he got worried. All sorts of dark thoughts flooded his imagination. Terrible images of her getting hurt or abducted.

Actually, he'd been far more worried and upset than her parents. Though they'd acted confused and dismayed, he'd always felt that they knew more than they'd let on.

Unhappy with their attitude, he took charge. He asked everyone if they knew what happened to her. He even looked for her himself, spending time and money that he didn't have in order to get her back. But his efforts had been in vain. She was gone.

He'd been devastated. After fueling his anger for a solid year, he found himself a new woman, Mary, and married her. Then, she got sick and died.

But then a miracle had happened. He'd overheard Julia's parents talking to one of their good friends in an aisle at the mercantile where he worked. During that conversation, they revealed that Julia had taken to writing to them every Christmas. In those letters, she shared news about her daughter.

His five-year-old daughter.

Ever since that moment, he decided he would do everything he possibly could to discover where Julia and their child was. Since he doubted she could have lasted more than a couple of months on her own, he needed to see the man she eventually married. To see who was raising his daughter as his own.

Then he would carefully tell them both how things were going to be.

Just imagining the alarm that would appear in her eyes warmed his insides. He would feel ten feet tall again, taking care to tell her man how she'd lain with him out of wedlock. How she'd betrayed him by running away. Then, he'd be sure to remind that man that leopards didn't change their spots. One day Julia would leave him, too, no doubt taking whatever children she'd given him as well.

Those warnings should be enough to convince her to give him back his daughter. If the Lord was going to take away his son, Luther was going to take matters into his own hands. He was going to have his child.

And if Julia tried to fight him? Well, he almost hoped she would.

Then he would deliver retribution. Then, he'd find peace and be himself again. He'd be able to stand a little straighter, knowing that he'd at last taken care of her selfishness. He'd at last get what was rightfully his.

"Good morning, Luther," Mr. Boysen called out.

Steadfastly pushing his dark thoughts away, Luther smiled at his boss. "Good mornin', sir. How are you this cold morning?"

"Better now that you are here." Looking him over, he grinned. "I hope you are feeling strong today."

"Yes, sir?"

"I decided that we need to expand our inventory. I found a mill out in Charm that has started to make some real fine ladder-back chairs. I want you to go with Bill to the mill and pick them up."

"Sure, boss."

"That ain't all, though. Kinsinger's makes some of the best finished wood for floors around. My wife decided that she wants a wood floor on our whole second floor, too. You and Bill are going to have to load up the wood for that."

"Yes, sir."

"Great. It's going to be a fairly long trip, so I told Bill that you should stop for lunch. It's on me."

Luther tipped his hat before taking a moment to give thanks to the Lord for the hard work. Between the long drive and the hard labor of loading the truck and unloading, he should be far too tired to worry about Julia or his missing daughter.

He'd have time to plot and plan tonight—seeing as he had nothing but time and space when he was alone at night.

Until he got her back.

Levi had looked out the window for Julia at least four times that morning. Shaking his head at his eagerness, he turned away and attempted to wipe off his kitchen counters again.

Unfortunately, they didn't look much better. Actually, they looked to be in sorry shape. For some reason, there was a film of some sort on the white laminate that soap and water couldn't penetrate. It was like there was some invisible barrier between it and the rest of the world that didn't want to be removed.

Kind of like how he'd been with his family, he supposed.

He was currently staying a bit apart from them. He didn't know if it was their obvious happiness, or the fact that each had moved forward to embrace the holiday season while he still couldn't seem to shake his feelings of grief.

Now, here he was, asking an obviously overworked widow to clean his house. A house that by all rights he shouldn't even have been living in.

It all made no sense.

But that didn't stop him from looking out the window for a fifth time. Or smiling when he saw Julia was walking up his short walkway, a canvas tote bag in one hand and a large basket that looked to be full of rags and cleaning supplies in the other.

Julia was wearing a dark-brown dress today. It peeked out under her black cloak with each step. It should have made her golden hair look paler or her pale skin void of color. But instead, the dark colors seemed determined to emphasize her fine features.

Levi rushed toward the door and opened it before Julia had the chance to knock.

"*Gut matin*," he said.

"*Gut matin* to you, too," Julia replied with a bright smile as she stepped inside. As he closed the door behind her, she set down her things and immediately began untying her black boots.

"There's no need to do that," he blurted. When

she looked at him in confusion, he explained. "The floors are in need of a good sweeping. You might as well keep your boots on and keep your toes warm."

But instead of heeding his advice, Julia simply unlaced her other boot and slipped it off. To his surprise, she was wearing green- and red-striped socks.

Unable to help himself, he grinned. "Those are mighty fancy."

She laughed. "They are fancy, indeed. But I can't fault them for that. These socks are favorites of mine, you see. A couple of years ago I taught an *Englisher* lady how to knit. She made me these as a thank-you present. They are warm and cozy and, well, festive. I pull them out every December."

"They are festive, to be sure." Feeling like he was about to say something inappropriate, like that he thought her feet looked kind of cute, he cleared his throat. "But these wooden floors are dirty. They're going to soil your socks."

"They probably will. But socks are meant to be washed." She shrugged. "I clean better with my heavy boots off."

Realizing it didn't really matter what she wore on her feet, he walked toward the kitchen. "Come on back, I have something for you."

After she slipped off her cloak and rested it on one of his two kitchen chairs, she gazed at the envelope he was holding. “Is that my payment for today?”

“*Jah.* It’s a hundred dollars.”

“That’s a lot of money for a job you haven’t seen me do.”

“I have faith that you will earn every penny of it.”

Continuing to stare at the envelope in a distrustful way, she said, “I should warn you that I’m gonna need to leave at one o’clock. I may not get everything done.”

“I don’t expect you will. Just write me a note and tell me when you can come back.” Then he handed her his key. “I figure you’re going to need this, too, to lock up. But there’s a problem. It’s the only key I have.”

“How are you going to get in?”

“You have two choices. You can either stop by the mill before seven and drop it off, or I can get it from you when I get home.”

“And when will that be?”

She sounded concerned. He had a feeling that she was regretting her decision to help him out. “Sometime around eight or so. Hey, is that too late?”

“It’s not. But will you be at work the whole time?”

“For most of it.” He looked at her intently. “Why?”

“It’s only eight a.m. now. If you don’t get

home until eight tonight, that's a twelve-hour day, Levi."

He still didn't understand her concern. "I know that."

A line formed between her brows. "But won't you be exhausted? I mean, I know it isn't any of my business, but it just seems like a long day."

It was. He needed to work long days so he would be exhausted and be able to sleep at night. He stayed at work so he wouldn't have to spend any more time in his house than he had to.

Afraid she'd somehow read his expression, he turned away so he wouldn't have to face her. "You know, you could always just set the key under the mat if you have plans for the afternoon and evening. Then you won't have to go to the mill. It's cold out and snowy, too. I don't want you to have to go to a lot of trouble."

"After I see Penny from school, she and I will walk to the mill and drop off the key. It won't be any trouble at all."

Looking at her again, he couldn't help but smile. "You sound sure."

"That's because I am sure. The walk will do us good."

"When you get to the mill, go to the main entrance. Right inside, you'll see a circular reception desk. My sister Rebecca will be there. You can give the key to her. She'll make sure to pass it on to me."

"I'll do that, Levi. Now, I had better get busy," she said with a smile.

Still a bit reluctant to leave her and feeling vaguely like he was abandoning a houseguest, he pointed to the teakettle that he'd placed on the counter next to the sink. "There's a chill in here. Since you are only in stocking feet, you might need something warm to drink. I picked you up a kettle so you can do that."

Her eyes widened. "You bought a kettle for me?"

"Well, *jah*. I couldn't have you worrying about heating water in one of my old pots or pans."

"*Danke*, Levi."

He waved off her thanks. "It's nothing. We sell them in our retail store. It was just a matter of picking one up." Crossing the kitchen, he opened a cabinet. "Here's where the instant coffee and tea bags are. I wasn't sure what you liked, so I got a couple of different choices."

She swallowed. "*Danke*," she whispered. "I canna believe you went to so much trouble for me."

He realized then that she was truly touched by his actions. It embarrassed him a little to see that something so small could mean so much to her. "Like I said, it was nothing. So, um, help yourself."

"I will do that . . . after I scrub that range," she teased.

He chuckled. "That might be a good idea."

She suddenly looked so jaunty, so sure of herself, he said, "You know what? I like you, Julia. You look like a timid thing, but there's something about you that's strong and mighty."

"Do you really think so?"

"I do."

Studying her, Levi wondered why she looked so surprised. Had no one complimented her on her personality before? Surely, her husband had told her the same thing often. He was tempted to tease her about that when he noticed that she had folded her hands in front of her. She looked prim and proper and ready for work.

"Is there anything in particular you'd like me to clean first?" she asked.

"Besides the range? *Nee.*"

"I'll just take things one step at a time, then."

Feeling almost tempted to pull up a chair and simply watch her fuss and clean, he grabbed his thick black coat from the back of a kitchen chair. "I, well, I'll get on my way and out of yours, then. I need to work and you . . . um, you have a lot to do."

The corners of her lips turned up just a touch. "Indeed, Levi."

"Yes." Looking at Julia standing in his house, her pretty face lighting up the dreary kitchen, he felt more than a little optimistic about life than he had in years.

After spending the last few months under a cloud of depression, the notion took him by surprise. Was he finally coming to terms with things?

He walked to the front room, grabbed his black wool stocking cap and gloves, then walked outside. The air was brisk and cold. A hint of blue sky was visible, but the light wind in the air signified that it wouldn't stay that way for long. Soon gray clouds would cover everything and bring with them the promise of another round of snow.

The change was inevitable, he mused. Funny how he was just understanding that.

Chapter 7

Tuesday, December 6

The moment Julia heard the front door close, she reached into her tote bag and pulled out a brand-new pair of yellow rubber gloves and some cleanser. Oh, but she'd feared Levi would never leave!

From the time she'd seen him watching her walk across the street to his house, she'd been a bundle of nerves. Levi affected her in a way no other man had before. He made her giddy and silly.

He made her want to forget how scared and alone she usually felt. He made her imagine that some men really were what they seemed to be.

Hoping to ease the worst of her nervous energy, she dampened a sponge, poured some cleanser on the top of the stove, and started working off what had to be years of grime.

Scrub, scrub, scrub. Rinse.

Over and over she repeated that pattern, scrubbing and rinsing and wiping. Little by little, the awful avocado finish on the stove began to gleam.

Pleased that she was making progress, she let

her mind drift toward Levi again . . . and the way she felt about him.

Her confused feelings only intensified when he'd opened the door for her, gave her too much money, and told her about his key.

She hadn't known how to respond to any of it.

Men in her life had never talked to her so openly before. She didn't know whether she should have quietly accepted his directions or voiced her opinion. She had the feeling that he would have welcomed her thoughts and maybe even appreciated her sharing more about herself.

But the memories of the way Luther had treated her ran too strong. He'd sometimes been friendly, almost kind. Then, the moment she'd think she could trust him, he would turn on her. He had mercurial moods, sometimes seeming weak and needy before igniting into anger when she tried to help him in any way.

Julia now knew that he'd done much of that on purpose. He liked making her wary. He enjoyed making her uneasy. It had almost been a game to him.

A terrible, cruel game that she'd knowingly participated in again and again. It was her fault that she hadn't seen him for who he was. Heaven knew, both her parents and her sister had tried to make her see him for who he really was.

By the time she'd left him, she was filled with regrets and deeply ashamed. Not only had she had sex before marriage, she'd disappointed her parents and no doubt shamed them and her sister, too. She had no one to blame for her problems and errors than herself, either. She'd been carefully brought up and taught right from wrong at a young age.

Her sister had been a wonderful-*gut* role model as well, both showing Julia the right way to act and offering advice when it came time to step out with eligible men.

But instead of taking Sarah's good examples to heart, Julia had ignored them all. She wasn't sure if it was the devil's doing, or plain laziness. Whatever the reasoning, she knew it was time to face the consequences.

It had felt like the rightful penance to change her name and carry her burdens on her own. So that was what she'd done. She had Penny in a free clinic and worked as much as she could. Over time, she grew to trust her employers, but she never looked at another man. She didn't dare let another man into her life and risk getting hurt again.

As time passed, she'd come to the conclusion that she'd likely never find a man willing to accept her or her past. She'd had a baby out of wedlock, never told the baby's father about Penny, and had even adopted an assumed name.

Furthermore, besides posting one note to her parents each Christmas, she'd abandoned them.

Who would ever welcome a woman who had done so many terrible things? No man she could imagine. Certainly not any man of worth.

She'd long ago accepted this, had been determined to simply be a mother to Penny and focus on a rather solitary existence. But in the two months that she lived in Charm, she'd made more friends than she had the entire time she lived in the motel in Millersburg.

Even more disconcerting was the fact that she was daring to trust others again. Honestly, it was as if her past had faded into practically nothingness! So much so that she was actually daring to imagine a future with friends, a husband, and more children.

Realizing she was sweating, she wiped her brow with the corner of her apron and reminded herself that such dreams would only bring her disappointment.

She should know better, too. Why, only she would dare to dream about having a man so opposite Luther. Only she would begin mooning over a man like Levi Kinsinger! He was handsome and athletic. Outgoing and friendly. He was also kind.

Then there was his standing in the community. He was one of the owners of a very successful business. He was well respected. No doubt he was wealthy. If he decided to go courting, there were likely many women who would be only too happy to welcome him into their lives.

He would never have to settle on a woman like herself.

She really, really needed to simply concentrate on cleaning his house.

Looking at the stove that was now sparkling clean, she tried to feel a sense of accomplishment. Tried to only care about how proud she was of her first task.

But all she seemed to summon was that it was just a clean stove. A clean, worn, ugly-colored stove.

It was nothing when compared to the man who owned it.

Pulling off her gloves, she groaned. Ack! Why was he constantly occupying her thoughts?

Because he was so different than Luther. Yes. That had to be it.

Frustrated with her drifting mind, Julia rinsed out the kettle he'd pointed out and filled it with water.

After lighting the gas flame, she forced herself to start concentrating only on the work that needed to be done.

She hadn't been lying when she said she only had until one o'clock to work on his house. Based on how dirty the stove was, she could probably spend every minute of her time in just this single room.

Feeling a little worried about the state of the rest

of the house, she decided to do a quick inspection first. Then she would determine where to start. With a feeling of dread, she walked down the hall to examine his bathroom. There was no telling what his shower tile was going to look like. She mentally prepared herself to see the worst.

Like her home, there were three doors down the hall. The first led to a small bedroom about the size of Penny's. But instead of housing a pretty twin bed with a brightly colored quilt across the top, only a few cardboard boxes and two empty duffel bags littered the floor.

The next door led to Levi's bedroom.

A king-sized bed hastily made stood proudly in the center of the back wall. Next to it was a beautifully finished bedside table made of cherry. Lining one of the plain white walls were a pair of laundry baskets that looked to be taking the place of a set of drawers.

Unable to help herself, she walked toward the bed and ran her hand along the smooth grain of the wood. It, too, was cherry. Oh, but it was a mighty fine piece of work. Obviously Amish-made, it was sleigh bed–style with an impressive head- and footboard. The wood was dark and rich. She couldn't help but think it seemed out of place in the small, rather dingy room.

To her surprise, Levi had made his bed neatly. Four pillows encased in white cotton lay across the top of a tightly tucked sheet, thick tan blanket, and a navy down comforter. The bedside table matched the bed and had two black iron knobs. On the table was a digital alarm clock, some pocket change, two handkerchiefs, and a flashlight.

The floor underfoot was scarred linoleum. It needed a good scrubbing. Actually, it needed to be replaced with hardwood. Yes, she could just imagine how lovely it would be when thick oak planks covered the floor. Then she would place a bright, merry rag rug in the middle. It would keep his toes warm when he woke up in the morning—

Keep his toes warm? She pressed her hands to her cheeks, embarrassed about the direction of her thoughts.

Quickly, she backed out of the room and opened the last remaining door.

And sure enough, she did have to brace herself, but not for the reasons she expected.

The bathroom was still faintly steamy and warm from Levi's morning shower. An underlying scent hung in the air, smelling of shampoo and soap and fresh cotton.

Closing her eyes, she realized it smelled of Levi. Just as she was inhaling deeply, she shook her head in dismay.

It had been less than five minutes, but here she was again, staring off into space and thinking about the man. He'd hired her to clean his house, not stand in each of his rooms and smell his scent!

Beyond embarrassed, she hurried back to the

kitchen. She was too warm to think about tea now. She turned off the stove, strode back to the entryway, and grabbed the rest of her cleaning supplies. She was going to tackle the bathroom first—and not because it vaguely smelled like him.

No matter what it took, she was going to have to keep her distance from him. She had secrets that couldn't be revealed and goals that needed to be attained.

It would be so terribly embarrassing if he ever guessed that he meant more to her than was seemly.

And she couldn't even imagine what he would say if he ever learned about her past. She hated thinking about what he'd say if he ever discovered how much she'd lied to him. No doubt he'd run as far away from her as possible.

That would hurt, of course. But she wouldn't blame him, either. Not one bit.

She'd long come to terms with the fact that she'd done what she did because she had no choice. And while others might have handled things differently, she'd done the best she could.

All that really mattered was that she'd kept Penny safe.

Yes, at the end of the day, Penny's safety was really all that mattered.

Chapter 8

❄ ❄ ❄

December 6

Levi had been in such a hurry to gain some space between himself and Julia that he hadn't taken the time to eat breakfast. He decided to grab something at Josephine's Café before heading into the mill.

"Hi, Levi," Josephine said merrily as he entered the cozy café, currently decked out in festive garland and red bows.

"Hiya, Jo. You're looking Christmasy in here."

"It's the season, you know," Jo replied with a smile. "I know you Amish like things plain, but I like a bit of whimsy in my life."

He grinned. "Amish or not, I think we could all use a bit of whimsy now and then. My *mamm* used to hang Christmas cards along the banister."

"That's a nice tradition. Then you can enjoy the cards all month long," she said as she grabbed a coffeepot. "Sit wherever you want and I'll bring you some coffee in a minute."

"Gotcha." Scanning the room, he was just about to settle on a table in the far back corner when he saw his sister Amelia and her fiancé, Simon, sitting near the window. When he grinned at them, Amelia waved him over.

As soon as he got to their side, Amelia raised her chin and beamed at him. “Hi, Levi. It’s good to see ya.”

Unable to help himself, he ran a finger along her cheek. “Hi yourself.” It was so good to see his sister so happy. “Seeing you both here is a nice surprise.”

Pulling out the chair next to him with one hand, Simon smiled. “Amelia and I are spending the morning together. After we eat, we’re going to go to The Refuge for a couple of hours.”

“I’m going to help Tess organize the kitchen,” Amelia said.

“I’m sure she’ll appreciate your help. You’re the most organized woman I know,” Levi teased. Turning to Simon, he said, “You’re not working today?”

“I’m taking the morning off. My team has everything handled and there’s nothing pressing going on.”

“Levi, listen to this,” Amelia said. “Tess received a visit from the police.”

“What?” Seeing Josephine approach, he held up a finger. “Hold on a minute. Hey, Jo, bring me some coffee, orange juice, and three fried eggs with sausage and biscuits, will ya?”

“Absolutely. Roast potatoes, too?”

“*Jah.*”

After Jo poured Levi some coffee, she left him. And he turned his attention back to Amelia. “Why were the police there? Did she have a problem?”

“I don’t think so,” Simon said. “But I want to make sure about that. She sounded kind of funny about the visit when I asked her about the cop coming over.” He sighed. “It’s one of the reasons we’re stopping by. I don’t think she told me the whole story.”

“Really?” Levi asked. “What do you think Tess could be hiding?”

Amelia smiled softly. “I have an idea.”

Simon rolled his eyes. “Oh, Amy.”

“What is your idea, Amelia?” Levi asked.

“Well, when Simon asked Tess about the officer’s visit, she just happened to describe the man’s brown eyes and wavy dark hair. Then she also confided that he was tall and strong.” Darting an amused glance at Simon, Amelia added, “This man also seems extremely capable.”

Levi stopped himself from grinning just in time. “Huh.”

“Yeah,” Simon grumbled. “That’s exactly what I thought.”

Since Levi was thinking that Simon’s sister was a bit infatuated with the cop who stopped by, he moved the conversation along. “Do you want me to go over there? I could talk to Tess for you. She might not want to tell her brother everything that was discussed.”

"*Danke*, but no. Our other brother Jeremy is supposed to show up, too. I'm sure Tess will explain everything when we're all together."

"Why are you eating breakfast now, Levi?" Amelia asked. "Isn't it a bit late for you to be heading to work?"

"Yeah, but I thought a meal out might do me good."

"I'm surprised you don't eat every meal here," she said. "I bet you aren't taking care of yourself."

"I'm taking care of myself just fine. You forget that I cooked for myself when I lived in Florida."

"Huh. Are you eating enough?"

"I hope so."

"You should come home. That house you've adopted is awful."

"There's nothing wrong with it. Jupiter Street ain't a bad place."

"There's not a thing wrong with Jupiter Street. But there's plenty wrong with your house. It's a mess." Brightening, she said, "I know! I'll go clean it after we visit The Refuge."

"*Nee*," Levi said at the same time that Simon did.

"Why ever not? I'm happy to help and I've got everything under control at the house."

"Please, Amelia," Simon said quietly. "I don't want you over there by yourself. I don't know all of Levi's neighbors."

His sister's blue eyes narrowed. "Simon, I

know you like to look out for me, but this is—"

"It's getting cleaned right now anyway," Levi said quickly, anxious to divert an argument.

"Oh?" Amelia asked. "Who did you find?"

"Julia Kemp. Do you remember meeting her at church?"

Amelia tilted her head to one side. "She's a little older than us, ain't so?"

"Maybe. She's a sweet thing."

"Is she, now?" his sister murmured.

"*Jah.* Pretty, too. She's about medium height, has blond hair and brown eyes. And a dimple. She has a way about her that is pleasing, too. So patient and kind." He picked up his coffee and took a fortifying sip, sure he was going to need it. So much for sounding like he hardly knew her!

And sure enough, there it came . . . but not from his sister, from Simon.

"Levi, you sound like you're interested in her."

"I'm not." Realizing with some surprise that he wasn't telling exactly the truth, he amended his words. "I mean, I don't think I am." When Simon peered at him more closely, he said, "I only asked her to clean my place."

"Out of everyone in Charm, why did you ask her?" Simon pressed.

Levi put his cup down, realizing with some surprise that Simon sounded almost upset that Levi had hired Julia. Weighing each word carefully, he said, "I asked Julia because she lives across the street, she wants the work, and I need the help."

"What do you know about her?"

"Not a lot. She's new to Charm and has a little girl."

"I do remember meeting Julia's daughter," Amelia said. "Her name is Penny. She's a sweet child."

"Do you know anything else about her?" Simon asked.

"Beyond that she's Amish? *Nee*."

Simon rolled his eyes.

Now Levi was getting irritated. "Do you care to tell me why any of this matters to you?"

"I'm only trying to look out for you."

"By warning me off pretty neighbors who like to clean?"

"By allowing people who you don't really know to be alone inside your house for hours at a time," Simon countered. "It's unwise."

"It's not like I have anything to steal. And even if I did, I doubt a woman like Julia would do anything like that."

"You are too trusting, Levi. Just because she seems like a nice lady doesn't mean you need to trust her so quickly."

Amelia looked concerned. "I've only talked to Julia at church, but she seems nice enough. I doubt she'd ever steal anything of Levi's."

"She won't," Levi said, not liking the fact that

Simon would even insinuate such a thing. "Plus, I have nothing to steal."

Simon exhaled just as Josephine approached with a tray of food. After passing out their three breakfasts, eggs for Simon and Levi, waffles and bacon for Amelia, Josephine topped off their coffee and departed.

When they were alone again, Simon spoke. "I'm not saying that she ain't a good person, but you don't know anything about her, do you?"

"She's new to town. I'm trying to get to know her."

"Just be careful. Take your time."

"Simon, I don't understand why you are saying such things. You are usually the most accepting person I know," Amelia said.

Simon looked down at his plate before replying. "I overheard her say something that struck me as strange. That's all."

"What did you hear?"

"I was in line, getting sandwiches after church, when I heard Mary Troyer asking Julia about her husband and his death."

"And?" Levi asked impatiently.

"She didn't have a good answer. She was vague and looked uncomfortable."

"Of course she was uncomfortable!" Amelia exclaimed. "If something ever happened to you, I wouldn't want to talk about it, either."

Simon's gaze softened on his fiancée before

meeting Levi's eyes again. "I might be wrong. I hope I am. But I've spent a lot of time avoiding questions about my past, Levi. I've also been around quite a few men and women who deliberately shrink from certain subjects for a good reason."

"That's not Julia."

Simon raised his hands. "Forgive me. I probably shouldn't have said a word. It's just that, well, you have been through a lot over the last couple of years. And, you are something of a catch, too. I've known more than one woman who didn't have much but was willing to do a lot of things for security, even lie about her past. Be careful."

Though Levi completely believed that Simon was jumping to conclusions—maybe even leaping to them—he also knew that his friend's concern came from the right place. "All she's doing is cleaning my house. That's it."

Amelia cleared her throat. "I hate to point out the obvious, but if Julia has had some pain in her past and is reaching out to Levi for help, we should count that as a blessing," she said softly. "Sure, Levi is a catch. But he's also got a good heart and would be a wonderful-*gut* friend."

Before Levi could comment on that, she turned to him and smiled. "Maybe that's why you decided to rent that awful house in the first place, Levi. Maybe the good Lord knew Julia needed a friend and He placed you nearby to be that friend."

His sister's words were sweet, but they also made him uncomfortable. "I wouldn't say that we were friends, or that we were united by divine intervention . . ."

"But it does seem like it was meant to be, don't you think?" Her bright-blue eyes gleamed.

Levi couldn't help himself. He chuckled. "I hope you don't use those eyes of yours on Simon too often, Amy."

"Why would you say that?"

"Because if you do, I bet he's putty in your hands."

"I would never flirt or blink my eyes to try to convince Simon to do something he doesn't want to do."

"Oh, yes, you do. And it works," Simon said, sounding both put upon and pleased by the fact.

Levi grinned at that . . . and couldn't resist needling his buddy a bit, too. "Do you do what all of us used to do when she stared at us that way?"

Amelia groaned. "Levi, *halt*."

Simon talked right over her. "Do what? Give her anything she wants? Of course I do."

Levi noticed Simon spoke without the slightest bit of sarcasm. He was serious. In response, Amelia tucked her chin and cut off another neat portion of her waffle, popping it into her mouth.

As for himself, he was torn between rolling his eyes at such devotion and saying a prayer of thanks. Amelia was the darling of their family. She was tenderhearted and far more shy and sensitive than the rest of the Kinsinger siblings. Levi knew he would have been unhappy if she'd ended up with a man who didn't treasure her.

Levi pushed his plate away, his breakfast only half eaten. While Amelia and Simon ate, he sipped his coffee and thought about Julia. She was a sweet woman. Kind to her daughter. Eager to be of help.

He wondered if Simon could possibly be right that she had something to hide. After all, she did seem awfully alone in the world. Most widows her age would live near family.

And most husbands he knew would have saved a good amount so their wives wouldn't be struggling to make ends meet the way she was.

It seemed there might actually be a mystery about her. It didn't make a lot of sense why she was currently making her way in the world with just one little girl by her side.

Now he had to decide whether he wanted to deepen their friendship and find out more about her . . . and then deal with what he discovered . . . or keep her as exactly what she was in his life: a pretty woman who was cleaning his house.

But he realized, right then . . . Julia Kemp was already far more to him than that.

He set his coffee cup down and felt like pressing his palms to his face.

"You okay, Levi?" Amelia asked.

"At the moment, I don't honestly know."

Chapter 9

❄ ❄ ❄

December 6

She hadn't meant to snoop. But when Julia had been cleaning Levi's countertops and attempting to put his snacks, his fruit, his wadded-up receipts and collected business cards, his pens and loose change into some kind of semblance of order . . . she came across a brochure for something mighty unexpected.

A colorful brochure about something called The Refuge.

At first she'd taken notice of the pamphlet because it seemed like an unusual thing for a man like Levi to hold on to. The brochure had photographs of children and women scattered through it. Most were not Amish, though there was a photo with the back of an Amish lady sitting in the corner of the room.

Levi was rough and tumble. He worked in a lumber mill and he was constantly surrounded by his many friends. She'd never seen him keeping company with Englisher children. With any children, for that matter.

She became curious, and before she knew it, she

was sitting down at his kitchen table, reading about The Refuge.

That was when she discovered that it was a meeting place for women and children who had been abused by loved ones.

Women like herself.

At last, she could admit it.

Her hands started shaking. Tears filled her eyes as memories, which she'd tried so hard to hold at bay, rushed forward, bringing back feelings of pain and embarrassment and helplessness. Each one was sharp and stung. Just as if she was still living that life with Luther. Just as if her shoulder was dislocated again.

Or she had a swollen cheek. A black eye. Bruised ribs.

Just as if Luther was hovering over her again as she lay on the ground, scared to move. Scared to do anything. All while both relishing and taunting her about her weakness.

Unable to help herself, she pressed her hands to her face. Even though she was willing them not to, pent-up tears kept forming in her eyes. She clenched her hands into tight fists as a cold sweat coated her spine. When her breath came in short gasps and her heart raced, Julia knew she was on the verge of having a panic attack.

Yet again.

"It's over," she whispered to herself. "You're

okay. Luther canna hurt you anymore. He doesn't even know where you are."

When she was able to move, she rushed to the sink and turned on the faucet. She splashed cold water on her face, not even caring that it coated her collar and the counter that she'd just wiped down.

The cold water helped. At last she felt like she could function again. She wasn't good, but she was well enough to continue her job.

Taking a deep breath, she glanced at the kitchen clock. Where had the time gone? It was already quarter to one! She now had only fifteen minutes to get to school to get Penny.

All she had time to do was stack Levi's papers in a corner, run to get her tote bag and carryall, and grasp hold of her cloak.

Though she'd known she wouldn't be able to finish all her work, things were far from the way she'd hoped to leave them. Nothing looked very spic and span.

Actually, it was rather untidy. The cushions of Levi's couch were still resting in the center of it. His broom was out of the closet, and two of his shirts were on his bedroom floor.

But she had no choice. As it was, she was going to have to practically run to get to the school on time.

She was simply going to have to apologize to Levi later. And she would. As soon as she got her bearings and could look at him without bursting into tears all over again.

After locking his door, she ran across the street to place her cleaning supplies next to her doorway, then darted down the street. At least the roads were clear of snow and the temperatures hovered around the freezing mark.

With the Lord's blessings, she might just make it to Charm School before Mrs. Mast began to get worried.

"Julia!" a voice called out just as she was speed-walking down Main Street. "Julia, is that you?"

Looking over her shoulder, she saw Darla Kinsinger. Last time they'd had church, she and Darla had struck up a conversation. That's when Julia learned that Darla was recently married to Levi's brother, Lukas. Once or twice she'd thought about mentioning Darla to Levi but decided against it. Discussing his sister-in-law felt a little pushy, almost like she was trying to form a close bond with him. Maybe she'd mention her new friendship with Darla if she and Levi got to know each other better.

Slowing down, she smiled hesitantly. "Hello, Darla. I'm sorry, but I canna stop to talk. I'm near out of time to get Penny."

Darla smiled. "No reason for you to slow down. I'm going to Charm School, too. I'm picking up my little sister, Gretel, today."

Relieved that she wasn't going to be the last

parent or guardian to arrive, she slowed her pace to match Darla's. "Aren't we late?"

Darla shrugged. "If we are, we're only late by five minutes or so. And you know how the end of the day goes. Rachel Mast chats with and hugs all the *kinner* as they leave. That always takes another ten minutes, at the very least."

What Darla said was true. There were many days that she'd stood in the school yard and waited for Penny to get one last hug from her teacher.

Why had she been in such a panic?

Because she'd been haunted by memories of Luther.

Pressing a hand to her heart, she exhaled and attempted to settle herself.

Darla noticed. "Is anything wrong?"

"*Jah.* I was worried I was going to be late."

"You're looking a little pale. Is that all?"

How could Julia respond to that? It wasn't like she could pour out her life story to Darla Kinsinger while they were walking to school! "It isn't all, but I was pretty worried. I didn't want Penny to have to wait for me."

Darla studied her before nodding. "I understand."

For some reason, Julia believed Darla did. "Do you know if the Kinsingers discourage visits to the mill?"

"Why? Do you need to talk to Rebecca?"

"*Nee.* Not her. I need to speak with Levi."

Darla slowed her pace to a crawl. "Levi?"

"*Jah.* I left your brother-in-law's *haus* in a terrible state. I was cleaning it when I lost track of time."

A slow smile lit her expression. "Hold on. You were cleaning Levi's grungy house?"

"*Jah.* He mentioned that he needed it cleaned." She smiled. "For you all, actually. And I needed some extra money for Christmas . . ." Here she went again, telling far too much about her personal life! It must be because she finally had found a home in Charm. She was comfortable here, almost as if she fit in.

Darla looked like she was trying hard not to giggle. After a few seconds, she said, "I'm sure he appreciates your efforts. Or will, when he sees them. We will, too. Every time Lukas and I try to go over to see him, he puts us off."

"His place is rather, um, dirty."

"Oh, I bet it is."

"He works a lot, you know."

Darla smiled. "As far as visiting at work? You and your daughter go on ahead. There aren't any rules like that. Kinsinger's is family owned, after all."

She exhaled in relief. "Thank you. He'd mentioned that I could drop off his key, but we didn't talk about me taking time out of his work. I don't want to cause him trouble. Or make him upset."

“Levi ain’t like that,” Darla said. “He’s a lot of things, but he’s kind and levelheaded. He doesn’t get upset easily, either. He won’t get upset with you.”

Julia didn’t need to be a mind reader to realize that Darla was attempting to tell her that she didn’t have to fear her brother-in-law. It was such a kind gesture, she almost smiled.

Instead, she nodded. “*Danke.*”

“You’re welcome. And look! Here come our girls, and it looks like they’re becoming friends, too.”

Becoming friends, too. Julia loved how that sounded. “I’m glad you called out to me, Darla. It was nice to walk with you.”

“I feel the same way,” she said as she raised her hand so the girls would see her and Julia standing off to the side of the playground.

But Gretel and Penny didn’t look like they were worried about seeing them at all. Instead, they were walking side by side and chatting in earnest about something.

“Gretel, I’m over here with Penny’s *mamm*,” Darla called out.

Looking pleased, they hurried over to meet them.

“Hiya!” Penny said. “Gretel and I stayed a couple minutes late to talk to Mrs. Mast.”

Julia bent down to kiss her daughter’s brow. “What were you girls talking with her about?”

"Christmas," Gretel said.

Darla and Julia shared a look. "I should have known," Darla said as she straightened the thick red knit scarf around Gretel's neck. "What were you talking about? What presents you were going to get?"

"Mmm-hmm," Gretel said. "And what I'm gonna make for you and Aaron and Hope and Samuel and Maisie and Evan and Patsy." After pausing for a much needed breath, she added, "And Lukas."

"*Jah*, we cannot forget Lukas."

Penny's eyes were wide. "You sure have a big family."

"I have six brothers and sisters plus a sister-in-law and a brother-in-law," Gretel said proudly.

"I only have a mother," Penny said.

Gretel's brown eyebrows rose. "That's it?"

"*Jah*."

Julia's heart broke as she listened to the longing in her daughter's voice. There wasn't anything to say about their situation, though. It was what it was. "Let's start walking, girls," Julia said, shrugging off Darla's sympathetic gaze. "We have things we need to do."

The girls started walking by their side. When they left the school grounds, Gretel blurted, "I don't have any parents."

"Darla ain't your *mamm*?" Penny asked.

Gretel giggled. "Of course not. She's my sister."

Eyes sparkling, she pulled on Darla's apron. "My bossy sister."

"That isn't true," Darla said, humor lacing her tone as they started down the path through two farms that was the shortcut toward town. "Your sister Maisie is bossier than me."

"I know Maisie," Penny said with a bright smile. "She knows everything at school."

Darla shook her head. "She likes to think she does."

"Is she coming along, too?" Julia asked.

"*Nee.* She left with her friends," Gretel said. "She is going ice skating today. That's how come Darla had to come get me. Maisie didn't want me to come with her, which isn't fair."

"You're too young, Gretel," Darla said. "You know that."

"I still count."

"That you do."

As the girls continued their conversation, chatting about Gretel's sisters and brothers and Christmas, and the fact that Evan always ate too many mashed potatoes, Darla grinned at Julia.

"Now you know what Patsy and Hope and I go through every day."

Julia was intrigued by how easy Darla made their unusual situation seem. "You and Patsy and Hope raise Gretel together?"

"I wouldn't say that. It's more of a group effort. Everyone in my family helps each other out. Patsy does a lot of the day-to-day tasks since Hope is engaged to my brother Aaron. See, Patsy lives at home. So does Aaron. I, on the other hand, live with Lukas at his house. Because of that, I try to pick up the slack when I can." She shrugged. "About one night a week I spend the night back at home, too."

"Without your husband?" Realizing that probably sounded a bit intrusive, Julia said, "Sorry. I'm just intrigued by how you all manage everything."

"You can ask me whatever you want. When Lukas and I finally got together, we decided to keep everything in our lives as open as possible." Lowering her voice, Darla said, "Before that, we used to keep far too many secrets. That hurt both of us."

Julia looked down at her feet. Of course Darla hadn't meant anything by her innocent comment, but it still stung. Her whole identity seemed to be composed of secrets. They were connected like a spindly spiderweb, loosely connected, sticky and deceptively hardy . . . but one that could also easily be torn down.

What would happen if her past came to light?

Her peaceful life could come crashing down.

"Julia, are you okay? Uh-oh, did I say something to upset you?"

Darla's sweet concern brought her back to the present. "Of course not. I guess my mind drifted."

"I'm not surprised. Our family is a lot to keep track of. I wouldn't have it any other way, of course, but when I talk about our logistics the way I just did with you, I realize that it all sounds kind of crazy."

"Not crazy at all. You're blessed to have so many people in your life to depend on. It's wonderful."

Darla eyed her carefully. "I bet it's hard sometimes, since it's just you and Penny. I would be lost without my family."

"Yes. Sometimes it is hard."

"Did your husband pass away a long time ago?"

Feeling like each word was in danger of getting stuck in her throat, she nodded and forced herself to continue. "He did. Soon after Penny was born."

"So she doesn't remember him?"

"*Nee.*"

"I am sorry." Her voice thick, she said, "I can't imagine how hard that must be on both of you."

Feeling like her spiderweb was mere seconds from falling apart and trapping her in its sticky strands, she tried to move the conversation along. "Like I said, it was a long time ago."

"Do you have parents to help you out?"

Again came another lie. "*Nee.*"

Julia couldn't help herself. She reached for her daughter and hugged her tight. "This has been quite the conversation," she said with as much cheer as she was able to muster. "But now we need to say goodbye. Penny and I have an errand to run."

Darla's blue eyes rested on her for a moment. "Like I said, I've had some difficult times, too. If you ever want to talk, or if you need something, all you have to do is ask."

"That's mighty kind of you." Feeling that lump in her throat, Julia said, "Sorry, but we really need to go."

"Of course. See you soon."

"Bye, Penny," Gretel said with a little wave.

While Penny waved goodbye to Gretel, Julia said, "Enjoy your weekend, Darla."

"I'll do my best," Darla said with a wry smile. "Hey, will we see you at church?"

"*Jah*. We'll see you Sunday."

"It's at the Reists' house. Not far."

"And it's supposed to snow on Sunday, so we'll get to walk in the snow," Gretel said. "That will be great fun."

Darla and Julia shared a wry smile. "*Jah*. I can't wait to shuttle everyone back and forth in the snow," Darla said with humor in her voice.

After they separated, Penny reached for her hand. "Where are we going now, Mommy?"

"Kinsinger Lumber," she said as they approached the attractive building that housed the showroom and offices of the large business. "I need to tell Levi something."

Penny's face lit up. "We're gonna get to see Levi?"

"We are. Well, hopefully we are. But you must be on good behavior."

"I will."

Her eyes widened when they came to the impressive front entrance. Cars filled the parking lot and several shoppers were bustling around them.

Julia wasn't sure why, but she felt nervous. She told herself it was because she was going to have to tell Levi that she didn't get very far in his house. That she was going to interrupt him at work.

That she was likely going to meet his sister Rebecca, who always seemed like one of the most confident put-together people Julia had ever seen.

Those were all good reasons to feel the flutter in her insides. Mighty good reasons.

So much better than the one she feared was the case.

Opening the door, she pasted a smile on her face, ushered Penny inside, and mentally prepared herself to act relaxed and as professional as possible.

Chapter 10

❄ ❄ ❄

December 6

"I wouldn't have thought the food here would be to my taste, but it's real good," Bill said to Luther as he wiped his mouth with his napkin.

Looking at his cleaned plate, Luther had to agree. After they'd spent over an hour loading up the chairs and the massive amount of wood into the back of the truck, Bill had pointed to a restaurant in Charm that looked like it could serve them right away.

Josephine's Café wasn't his normal type of place. It was small, had brightly painted walls and all kinds of artwork hanging, most of which looked to be made by children. It also had mismatched tables, mismatched glassware, and checkered tablecloths. But the woman who owned the place had seemed nice enough, and the menu sounded good. She had three soups on the menu as well as chili and two meals with chicken.

He ordered cream of broccoli soup and chicken with mushrooms and rice. It was hot and delicious. He ate with a true appreciation, hardly stopping to talk. Luckily, Bill did the same.

When they were done, both men leaned back in their chairs with a satisfied sigh. The server brought them thick mugs of freshly brewed coffee and they were enjoying the warm drink before going back out into the cold.

"I'd come to Charm every week if we get to eat here," Luther said. "This is the best meal I've had in a long time. Years, even."

Bill grinned. "I was just thinking the same thing. My wife is a good cook, but not this good." Looking at him carefully, he said, "I guess you don't get a chance to eat a lot of home-cooked meals anymore. I sure am sorry for your loss."

With effort, Luther tried to look remorseful. "*Danke.* I appreciate you saying that. Mary wasn't a good cook, but her efforts were better than what I am able to rustle up these days."

"How long has it been?"

"A year. She died last December, right before Christmas."

"That's hard." Bill looked increasingly uncomfortable. No doubt he regretted bringing up the conversation in the first place. "Perhaps in time your pain will ease."

"I am sure it will. The Lord has seen to give me many obstacles over the years, some were worse than others. But still, I have survived."

"You have, indeed. That's a blessing."

Luther nodded again. He was glad he had survived. Glad he'd survived Mary's failures and

Julia's departure. He'd been betrayed by two women, which was definitely two women too many. He intended for that to be the last time a woman caused him so much pain.

Tossing his napkin on his lap, Bill looked around. "Well, I better ask for the check and hit the bathroom. We're gonna have to get on our way soon. It's a long drive back to the store, and we're gonna have a lot to unload. If we want to get home before six or seven, we're going to have to move fast."

"When the server comes back, I'll ask for the check."

"Thanks."

The server did walk by but Luther didn't signal her. He wanted another moment to sit and stare out the window. He figured there was nothing wrong with sitting for another couple of minutes. He worked hard, really hard. By his way of thinking, he didn't earn enough for his hours, either. He deserved these few minutes of rest. As Bill had said, soon they'd be carrying around pallets of flooring.

He sipped his coffee and gazed out the window. Charm was a picturesque place, to be sure. The rolling hills, now covered with snow, looked pristine. No doubt in the spring and summer they'd be covered in vibrant green. Absently, he watched several couples walk by on the sidewalk that lined the restaurant.

Some were Mennonite, others were Englishers. There were several Amish men and women, though. He was wondering why so many people lived in town when he remembered glimpsing into the Kinsinger showroom. It had been packed with people and merchandise.

When Bill had commented on it, Rebecca the receptionist chuckled and said that everyone was busy shopping for Christmas. Her expression and voice had been filled with pride.

He supposed most people did only have shopping and gift giving on their minds. After all, December wasn't the source of pain for everyone like it was for him.

"You got the check?" Bill said.

Luther jerked away from the window. "Huh?"

"Come on, man. We've got to get on the road. Mr. Boysen ain't going to like us dawdling."

He stood up. "Sorry. I guess I had too much to eat."

"Well, hit the bathroom if you need to. I'll pay."

"Sure." After apologizing again, he glanced out the window, just to see some more of the snow falling.

Then froze.

There, walking by, was a woman who looked very much like Julia. And she was holding a little girl's hand.

He stepped closer to the glass, nearly placing his palm on the pane.

He felt frozen and almost as if he'd stepped into a fog, hardly able to completely comprehend what he'd just seen.

Could his quest to discover what had happened to Julia and his child really be this easy? Had he just seen his daughter? He hadn't gotten a good look, but she had looked to be about five years old. She also had thick golden hair. And brown eyes.

Just like the woman who held her hand.

Just like Julia.

He was almost positive it had been them. And with that, he realized that the Lord must have been on his side, too. Surely, He had been guiding him this whole time, directing him to work at the general store, to be with Bill at Boysen's Mercantile.

He was so grateful. So thankful. So much so, he was tempted to kneel down on this knees right then and there and praise the Lord for being so true and good.

But just as suddenly, anger and frustration bubbled up inside him as well. Yes, he had seen them, but they were still not in his grasp. And they'd been away from him for years.

All because of Julia's subterfuge.

He clenched his fists. How could a man expect to be calm when he was faced with all he had lost?

"Luther, I'm serious," Bill called out from the

doorway, his tone filled with impatience. "We have to go. Get a move on while I warm up the truck."

Only by sheer force of will did Luther turn away. He needed this job. More importantly, he needed the transportation to Charm. If Julia was indeed hiding here, he would find her.

He was smart and he was determined. She was neither of those things.

However, she could cook. She was a hard worker, too. And, until she'd run from him, easily managed.

Maybe after he took the child back he would allow Julia to come along. She could live in his house and care for the girl and cook and clean for him, too.

He wouldn't marry her, of course. She didn't deserve that much respect.

But if she wanted to stay with his daughter and take care of her while he was working, he would allow her to do so.

Imagining how he could use her love for the girl to his advantage, he began to see the possibilities. There were no doubt many things Julia would be willing to do in order to keep the girl nearby.

And because of that, there were many ways he could think of to make her pay for his pain and suffering. So many, he would almost enjoy it.

Chapter 11

❄ ❄ ❄

December 6

Volunteering to mentor Peter Schlabach had been a good decision, Levi decided as he watched the boy handle the new tool with more confidence as each minute passed. The teen's eagerness and enthusiasm was a good reminder of the way he'd been when his father had first allowed him to work at his side.

Because Levi was four years younger than Lukas, he didn't have quite the same memories of their father the way his brother did. Many of his strongest memories of his *daed* revolved around his childhood and teens. Times when his father had been his disciplinarian and guide.

When Levi had started working at the mill, he'd been more anxious to fit in with the rest of the workers and not be seen as simply the boss's son.

He'd also spent quite a bit of time acting up and joking around, anxious to not be compared to his serious older brother. Now that he looked back on those days, he imagined his father had felt more than a little dismayed by his younger son's behavior and actions.

When Levi was in Pinecraft working on a crew, he'd realized that he'd spent far too much time worrying about how others perceived him. Especially since it didn't really matter. He was his father's son, just as Lukas was. There was no escaping that, he knew that now.

He'd been proud to be a Kinsinger. Now he would give anything to tell his father that he'd been proud to be his son.

Perhaps that was why he'd jumped at the chance to mentor Peter. At just fourteen, he was going to spend the majority of his time at Kinsinger's running errands or working in the mailroom. But little by little, he would learn how to work the machinery that they used.

Levi was ready to honor his father by passing on some of the skills that his *daed* had once shared with him. Although his father would never be able to see Levi follow in his footsteps, Levi liked to think that he would have been pleased.

So far, mentoring Peter had been anything but a disappointment. He'd enjoyed the boy's company, found his sense of humor to be dry and amusing, and respected his work ethic.

Levi was also certain that Peter was going to be a fine addition to the lumber mill's workforce. The boy had good instincts and a fine sense of what worked and what didn't.

He practically held his breath as Peter made one more pass, then carefully turned off the machine.

After blowing away the sawdust from the plank of wood, Levi felt more than a small amount of pride. Watching Peter's accomplishments truly was more enjoyable than experiencing his own.

After they removed their safety goggles and earplugs, Levi moved to one side.

"There you go, Peter," Levi encouraged as he looked over the teenager's shoulder. "That's the way to finish the edges of each shelf." Running a finger along the edge, he said, "Look how even you made this. I couldn't have done better myself."

"Are you serious?"

"Absolutely. I don't fib when it comes to work."

"Thank you, then." Peter beamed. "I've been working hard. I want to get better."

"You are."

"This tool ain't hard to use, as long as you go slow." Looking up, he added, "Roman said that going slow in here is better than fast."

Looking at the sander, he nodded. "I reckon you're right. You can always take away some wood or smooth it out, but if it's gone, it's gone. And that can be costly."

"I don't want to be the one costing you money, Levi."

"Me, neither," he teased. "I'm supposed to be teaching you how to do a good job." Levi didn't have the heart to tell him that every one of them was probably guilty of ruining a perfectly good piece of lumber at least once in their lifetime. "In any case, I was serious. You are doing a good job with that sander. Some men don't have the patience."

Peter grinned. "If you happen to see my father, tell him that I'm real patient, will ya? He's always saying I rush too much."

Levi grinned. "I'll be glad to pass on the praise." Peter's father was one of their most trusted employees, but he was one of the managers of the retail shop, not a craftsman. Though he'd never said anything, Levi imagined that Peter's father had worried about his son doing a good job in the actual mill. "And don't worry about your father chewing on you about things. My *daed* seemed to end each day with a long list of things I could have done a better job with. It's the way of fathers and sons, I think."

"If you got a talking to, it was no more than the rest of us," Rebecca said as she strode toward them. "Our parents were equal opportunity chewers."

Peter stood up a little straighter as he smiled at Rebecca. "Hi."

She smiled softly. "Hello, Peter. And before you ask, Lilly is doing just fine today."

"Tell her I said hi and that I'll be by after work."

"I'll do that. She told me that you're taking her out for a sleigh ride this weekend. I'm jealous. I haven't been on a sleigh ride in ages."

Levi winked at Peter. "You are sure making the rest of us men look bad, son. I hear you're always taking Lilly on all kinds of fun activities."

"A group of us are going," he said quickly. "My *daed* has been helping me fix up the sleigh."

"Don't let Levi's teasing bother you. I just wanted to share that it's practically all Lilly can talk about. She can't wait."

Levi grinned at his sister. Rebecca's stepdaughter was Peter's girlfriend, and the boy was unabashedly devoted to her. "You out making rounds, Beck?"

"Actually, I came to get you," she said with a new lilt in her voice. "You have some visitors."

"Who is here?"

"Julia Kemp and her daughter, Penny." She waggled her eyebrows at Peter. "Both seemed pretty eager to see you."

Peter's eyes lit up. "You courting, too, Levi?"

Whether it was because Rebecca was looking at him like she knew a big secret or because Peter looked so surprised, Levi felt his skin heat up. "I am not," he responded with a little too much force. "Julia is my neighbor. And she's been cleaning my house. No doubt she came over here to talk about that."

"Oh. Sorry," Peter said quickly.

Rebecca's brows rose and immediately Levi felt bad. Though there wasn't a thing wrong with being a housekeeper—it took skills he wasn't sure he had ever possessed—it didn't seem right to simply classify the lady like that. "She's a friend, too. A good friend."

"Well, her daughter is adorable. Practically bouncing on her toes, she's so excited to see ya."

That news made him happy, though he wasn't exactly sure why.

"Give me a sec and I'll walk with you," he said to Rebecca before turning to Peter. "You've got a choice. You can take a break now or work on those shelves by yourself."

"You'll trust me to use the sander on my own?"

The boy's eyes were practically shining. This time, he didn't even try to hide his pleasure. "I trust you, Peter. But I feel like I should remind ya that these shelves aren't practice scraps. The customer is paying good money and he expects good quality. If you mess them up, no one is going to be happy."

Looking completely somber, Peter nodded. "I understand."

Levi patted him on the shoulder. "I'm good with whatever decision you make. Either way, if I'm not back by the time Roman wants you, don't forget to clean up the area."

"I won't forget."

Once he turned his back and met Rebecca's gaze, Levi winked. Rebecca smiled at Peter before walking by Levi's side to the door.

Only when they were outside, walking quickly

through the cold before entering the main building, did Rebecca speak. "What do you think Peter is going to do now that he's on his own?"

Levi waited until they walked inside again to answer. "I'm guessing that he will sand those shelves and probably do a real fine job of it."

Rebecca slowed her pace. "He's still young, Levi. Maybe it isn't safe for him to operate a power tool on his own."

"I don't think he could hurt himself too bad if he tried. Plus, he's been using the sander by my side for over a month now. I'm also confident that he's going to be more careful on his own than if I was watching him."

"You look mighty pleased by that." She eyed him curiously as they passed a series of bulletin boards and a water cooler.

"I am. He's a good worker and smart as a whip. He's going to be an asset to Lukas for many years to come."

Right before they entered the main lobby, Rebecca stopped. "You mean an asset to you and Lukas, right?"

"*Jah*. And to you, too," he teased. "It's a family business. Ain't so?"

"Levi, *nee*."

He raised his eyebrows. "No?"

"You know what I'm talking about, Levi. You are talking as if you don't run this company, too."

Realizing that her words were exactly what he'd

been thinking just a few minutes earlier, he attempted to keep his voice even. "You and I know that Lukas is the true head of the Kinsinger mill. It's always been that way."

"But it doesn't have to be."

"Becky, I'm okay with that," he said softly. "I am proud to be a Kinsinger and I'm proud to help as much as I can. There ain't a man here who isn't aware of that. But Lukas is in charge. It's a good fit for him."

Her eyes widened. "Hold on, now. We should talk more about this."

"Maybe so. But not right now. Right now I've got a lady and her daughter to see."

"That's another thing we should probably talk about."

"If you want to talk, I'll talk. But not right now," he called over his shoulder as he walked into the lobby.

And then, there they were.

Unable to help himself, Levi paused for a moment and studied them. Julia and her daughter were sitting side by side on a decorative bench near the entrance to Lukas's office. Julia was still in her brown dress, though a jaunty red wool scarf was now wrapped around her neck. By her side sat Penny, dressed in a dark-pink dress, thick black tights, boots, and a matching red scarf. Her feet were swinging in motion to some song or beat that must have been playing in her head.

Both of them were gazing at Mercy intently.

And Mercy, their eighteen-year-old fill-in receptionist, was putting together a gingerbread house. Just like no one did anything else around a lumber mill than glue cookies together with white icing.

After giving Rebecca a curious look about Mercy's craft project, he strode toward Julia and Penny. "Hi, ladies. You didn't have to stay after you dropped off the key."

Julia got to her feet. "I wanted to mention something to you, as well. I'm mighty sorry to interrupt your work."

"It's no bother. I'm glad you're here." Leaning down, he smiled at Penny. "You two have brightened my day."

"I like it here," Penny said with a cute smile.

Visibly collecting herself, Julia said, "I wanted to let you know that I didn't get as far as I would have liked on your house. I'm sorry about that, it wasn't my intention to leave a job unfinished."

Boy, she seemed nervous. Treading carefully, he decided a light touch might be the best way to get her to relax. After all, the Lord knew that he was the last person to complain about another person cleaning. "It was that messy, huh?"

"I wouldn't call it messy as much as in need of a good cleaning. I could go back to your house now and finish the job . . . if you don't mind Penny being with me."

He was very aware of Rebecca and Mercy eavesdropping unabashedly on the conversation. It made the topic—his messiness and her cleaning that messiness—feel like it was even more intimate than it was.

To his dismay, he felt his cheeks heat. He hoped he wasn't blushing because he couldn't remember the last time he had done that.

"There's no need for that," he said awkwardly.

Her eyes widened. "Why, there most certainly is. I don't want to leave a job unfinished."

"Of course not. But you have Penny with you now." Leaning toward her, he added, "Watching your mother clean sounds pretty boring. Ain't so?"

But instead of agreeing with him, Penny looked slightly worried.

"She'll be fine," Julia said. "She's used to watching me work."

For some reason, that statement broke his heart. Julia really did have her hands full, and it was now apparent that this wasn't a new development, either.

Currently, he was aware that she worked at the notion shop, took care of her daughter on her own, and now cleaned his house for extra money. Through it all, he'd yet to hear her complain or sound like she was feeling sorry for herself.

He noticed then that her free hand was clenched into a tight fist. Was she worried that he was going to be mad at her? Or worried that he would tell her no?

"How about you stop by on your next day off, next week, and continue where you left off?" he said slowly. "That will suit me fine."

"You should take him up on the offer," Rebecca interjected. "Levi's always been untidy. He never did like to make his bed or pick up his clothes off the floor. It was a problem even when he was a little boy."

He groaned and glared at his sister. Hopefully, she was going to realize exactly what he was irritated about and stop making him sound like a spoiled toddler. "Really, Becky?"

"Oh, don't act so surprised," she retorted with a wave of her hand. "It's true. You know it is."

"It's not that true."

" 'Course it is. Even Amelia had a time getting you to clean off the sink when you were done in the bathroom before you left for Florida." Turning to Julia, she said, "He left razor stubble all over the countertop."

When Mercy giggled before hastily covering her mouth, Levi couldn't imagine the situation getting any worse.

Then, of course, his brother had to walk toward the doorway of his office. "What's this I'm hearing that involves Levi and bathroom sinks?"

"Nothing," Levi said firmly.

Rebecca leaned against the front of her reception desk. "We were just discussing what a mess our little brother was."

Lukas grinned as he joined them. "It's true. He was like that from birth. I hated sharing a room with you. Once I even asked Mamm if I could switch with Rebecca and share a room with Amelia."

Just as if he wasn't there, Rebecca gasped. "*Nee*, you did not."

"Of course I did. Amelia went to sleep early, never complained, and was neater than the three of us combined. You got off easy, Beck."

Julia looked down at her feet and smiled.

"We really don't need to review our childhood antics in front of half the company, Lukas," Levi said.

"It's only me," Mercy chirped. "And I think it's funny. I knew I'd love working the reception desk. One really does learn all sorts of things."

For the first time, Rebecca looked a bit embarrassed.

As did Lukas. "I hope you will not use this as fodder for conversation, Mercy," he said.

"Oh, *nee*, Lukas. I wouldn't do that."

Turning to Julia, Lukas held out a hand. "Hi there. I don't know if we've ever met," he said to Julia. "I'm Lukas Kinsinger."

Julia looked like she'd just seen the governor

enter the shop. She was all wide eyes. "I know who you are. I'm Julia Kemp. This is my daughter, Penny."

"Pleased to know you. Did you, ah, need some help in the retail store?"

"She didn't come in to shop. She came here for Levi," Mercy explained.

Before Levi could speak for himself, Rebecca continued. "*Jah.* They're Levi's neighbors. And Levi even asked her to clean for him."

"That's great, considering we're all supposed to come over soon," Lukas said. "I can't wait to see all what you've done to it, Levi."

There was no mistaking Lukas's sarcasm. And while Levi was willing to put up with being teased about his slovenly housekeeping, he wasn't willing to discuss his rental house in the reception area of the mill. "Watch it, Luke."

Julia looked from Rebecca to Levi to Lukas. "I'm sorry. I didn't mean to disrupt everyone's work. I just had to talk to Levi about something. But we're done now. Um, what you suggested will be just fine, Levi."

Staring at Mercy, who had gone back to carefully putting together the gingerbread house, Lukas said, "I hate to point out the obvious, but it don't look like there's a lot of work going on at the moment."

Mercy, who was holding two pieces of gingerbread, with some thick white icing that looked hard enough to break two teeth, froze. "Are you referring to me, Lukas?"

"Anyone else making gingerbread houses around here?"

She rolled her eyes. "This is work. We sell these kits. I'm making a model. Models help the customers, you know."

"I bet they do at that," Rebecca said.

"I was in the middle of it when Rebecca asked me to watch the reception desk."

Julia turned to the bench and picked up her black cloak. "Obviously, I'm disturbing people right and left. I think I'll let you all get back to your jobs."

"Hey, wait a minute. Are you in a hurry?" Rebecca asked. "Because we have hot cocoa and cookies in the café upstairs." She pointed over to a balcony where the small café was indeed open. Smiling at Penny, she said, "Everyone needs to take time for cookies and cocoa."

"Can we have some, Momma?" Penny asked.

"I'm afraid now isn't a good time. Everyone here has a lot to do."

Just as Rebecca was about to invite her, Levi jumped in. "I'm not too busy for cookies. Come with me, I'll take you both up now."

Still looking unsure, Julia shook her head. "There isn't a need . . . and besides, it's not like today is a special occasion."

"Cookies and hot cocoa aren't for special days.

I think they're perfect for any occasion." Looking at Rebecca, he said, "Right, sister?"

She grinned. "Absolutely."

Seeing that Julia was wavering, he said, "Now's a perfect time. I promise, I was ready for a break now anyway."

"If you're sure?"

"I'm sure."

"All right. *Danke.*" Picking up her and Penny's cloaks, she smiled at her daughter. "This will be a real treat for us. Right, Penny?"

"Uh-huh." To Levi's surprise, Penny walked over to him and held out her hand. "What kind of cookies are up there?"

Wrapping his big palm around hers, he looked down into her expectant expression and felt his heart melt a little bit. "I couldn't begin to guess. But let's go see."

Then, because there didn't seem to be any other way to handle it, he led Penny past the reception desk, and past Lukas standing by his door, and up the stairs. Julia was just steps behind.

Once they got to the café, he released Penny's hand and took the cloaks from Julia, setting them on an empty chair at one of the tables near the balcony railing. "I'm sorry about all that," he said. "I would tell you that I'm surprised by my brother and sister getting into my business, but I'm not. They love to stick their noses where they don't belong."

"They didn't bother me. I just hated to see that I was disturbing everyone."

"You didn't. It's busy around here, but mainly in the retail area. The front office is a little quieter than normal in December. A lot of people who Lukas and Rebecca deal with are either on vacation or too busy with their own businesses to deal with ours."

"Oh."

Realizing that he'd just given her a lot of information she hadn't asked for, he added, "What I'm trying to say is that I'm glad you stopped by. You never need to worry about coming over here."

"I understand." Looking a little sheepish, she added, "And I'll also stop apologizing."

"*Gut.* Now, let's go see about that hot chocolate and cookies, Penny."

Penny hurried to the counter and stood up on her tiptoes.

"We've got sugar cookies and blond brownies today," Clara, the sweet-tempered café manager, said. "Either of those sound tasty, dear?"

Penny looked at her mother.

Julia smiled sweetly. "Choose whichever one you want."

"The sugar cookie, please," Penny said.

Joining her at the counter, Levi pulled out his wallet. "Give me two of each, Clara. And three hot chocolates."

"Sure thing, Levi. You go sit down and I'll bring them to ya."

After they sat down, Julia waved a hand around the room. "This is so nice."

"I think so, too. It was my father's idea to put a café in. Customers like it and Clara's family has been managing it for years. It's good for them, too."

"The mill is such a big place."

"It really is." He couldn't resist bragging a little. "We have over two hundred employees and eight buildings. This showroom is over twelve thousand square feet."

"And it's your family's business, too. You must be so proud to have such a legacy."

"I am," he said, realizing that he hardly spent much time thinking about his legacy anymore. Instead all of his focus had been on work and trying to overcome his grief. "You know, after the fire last year, I've been having a difficult time. My father's death hit me hard."

"Of course it did."

"I've not only missed him, but I've been trying to figure out where my place is in the family's business."

Julia's expression was full of sympathy. "Have you come to any conclusions yet?"

"I think so. I still have a lot to figure out, but I have finally remembered one very important thing."

She leaned forward. "What was that?"

"That even if both of my parents died far too young . . . I was blessed to have them. I'm blessed to have my siblings and this business, too." Shaking his head, he said, "I never thought I took any of this for granted, but I don't think I ever fully appreciated all that the Lord has given me."

"I've had moments like that, too," she said, looking at Penny, who was now standing at the balcony, watching all the people below like they were animals at the zoo. "Penny makes my life wonderful."

"She's so cute. I bet she does."

"Here you all go," Clara said. "Three hot chocolates and two of each kind of cookie."

Penny turned around in a flash. "Which one is mine?"

Clara pointed to the one with both whipped cream and crushed peppermint on the top. "This one, of course."

Penny gazed at it with wide eyes. "*Danke.*"

Julia shared a smile with Levi. "I don't think Penny or I will ever forget this visit."

Her comment was sweet and dear. Just like her look of happiness.

Something was brewing between the two of them that had never happened before. There was an awareness there, a sense that there could be something more between them if the Lord gave them time.

He was enjoying the experience of forming a bond with the sweetest woman he'd ever met.

It was amazing how the Lord worked. Just as he'd come to terms with being a bachelor for another couple of years, just as he'd given up on ever finding a woman who was trustworthy and kindhearted, he'd found Julia. The fact that she came with a cute little girl named Penny . . . ?

That was a wonderful thing.

Chapter 12

❄ ❄ ❄

December 6

Tess was sitting on the floor of the main room of The Refuge and having the time of her life. Playing Legos with a little four-year-old boy did that to a person.

Tucking her knees under her, she held up the bright blue and red building she'd just constructed. "What do you think, Scott? Will this be a good barn?"

He giggled. "No."

"No?" She raised her brows in mock alarm. "Why ever not?"

He giggled again. "Because it's too small," he said. "It won't even hold a pig." Reaching into one of the pockets in his jean overalls, he pulled out a small plastic pig. "See?"

Carefully, she took the little pink pig and put it in the middle of her barn. "My barn holds one pig. What's wrong with that?"

As she hoped, he laughed even more uproariously, the way only small children seemed to be able to do. "You can't just have one pig, Tess."

"Really? How come?"

"Because they're gonna get lonely, that's why," he said with complete confidence.

"I guess you have a point," she murmured as she watched him construct a building of his own.

Scott's mother Beth had knocked on the front door at seven that morning. Still a little bleary from sleep, Tess had let her and her little boy in, then felt like crying when she saw the condition the mother was in. When she admitted that her boyfriend had hit her, Tess helped her to sit down and cared for her face.

Then she'd listened to Beth's story while making her and Scott some toast and cereal. They'd been hungry, eating the humble meal with so much care and gratitude that it nearly broke Tess's heart. Only after Tess had shared some of her own experiences did Beth allow Tess to call Officer Perry. Luckily, he was able to come right over.

Now Beth had been talking at the kitchen table with both Officer Perry and Julianne, the social worker, for the last hour.

Tess wasn't sure what was going to happen next, but she felt a warm glow of satisfaction knowing that Beth had even known to come to The Refuge in the first place. She'd slowly confided that a woman she'd met at a shelter had told her about Tess and The Refuge. Beth shyly admitted that she had come, hoping the reality really would be as safe as she'd been led to believe.

That one statement brought tears to Tess's eyes. She felt validated. Indeed, she had been right to open this space. Absolutely right. There was a need for The Refuge, even here in the middle of Amish country.

She was just about to tease Scott a little bit more when he stiffened next to her. Tess looked up and saw his mother, Julianne, and Officer Perry standing nearby.

Hoping to ease his discomfort, Tess held up the pig. "Scott here is so smart," she told them. "He's just been telling me about how we need to rebuild my barn."

As Scott's shoulders relaxed, his mother's tremulous smile grew larger. "Thank you for playing with him."

"No need to thank me. I've been having a great time."

Julianne knelt down next to them. "Scott, come sit with your mommy and me, okay?"

After Tess nodded, Scott stood up and walked to his mother's side.

Then, to her surprise, Officer Ken took Scott's place on the carpet. After resting his hands behind his back, he looked at her closely. "You okay?"

"I'm fine." Lowering her voice, she confided, "I'm worried about Beth and Scott, though. They were so hungry. I think they've had quite the time of it."

"I'm worried about them, too. However, I've

got a feeling that things are about to get better for them."

His eyes were warm, like he was holding on to a good secret. "Really? What happened?"

"Beth confided that a couple of her friends had been trying to convince her to get out of the relationship she was in. She just called one of them and asked for help."

"And?"

He grinned. "Beth and Scott are going to go over there. Her girlfriend promised that they could take her guest room and stay there for a couple of months."

"That's awesome."

"I thought so, too. Julianne is going to give her a ride in a little bit."

"I can't believe it all worked out so well."

Picking up a Lego brick, he rolled it between his fingers. "I can, but I am just as pleased about it as you are. Beth has a long way to go, of course. She needs to gain some confidence, and she needs to get some counseling. There's even a chance that she'll go back to that creep. But she seems determined to do the right thing for herself and her boy. That says a lot."

Remembering how long her own road had been, she nodded. "I think a person has to start somewhere. And that first step is usually the most important one."

Officer Perry tossed the Lego into the bucket.

"Yep, we're going to have to sit back and wait. For now, we've done all we can do. That said, I don't see too many cases like this get solved so easily. It's made me feel like we really can make a difference in people's lives if they give us a chance. Today's meeting has been a blessing for me."

She liked how he talked like they were working together. As if she, too, was helping that mother. She also really liked that he called what was happening a blessing. It was important to her that he didn't think it was just luck. She truly believed that the Lord had been on her side all of her life.

And she liked his kind dark-brown eyes, too.

So much so that she decided to take a chance. "Officer Perry, I was going to make some chicken chili and corn bread on Friday night. Any chance you'd like to come back here for supper?"

A look of surprise crossed his face before he smiled slowly. "If I say yes, would you call me Ken?"

"Yes."

He looked even more pleased. "What time?"

Now that it was really happening, she became a little flustered. "Maybe six? Or is that too early? I have no idea what time policemen end their days."

"I have an early shift on Friday, so six sounds perfect. See you then," he said as he stood up.

Less than thirty minutes later, Tess was hugging

Beth and Scott goodbye and smiling shyly at Ken as he told her he'd bring over some ice cream for them to share after her chili.

The moment the door was closed, she ran to the kitchen, did a little inventory, then threw on her coat and boots and walked to the small grocery store nearby.

Just as she was looking at the selection of peppers and was wondering just how spicy she should make her meal, she spied her brother and Levi Kinsinger across the aisle.

She hurried over to them. "Look at us, Simon!" she said. "We're meeting in the grocery store."

He grinned at her exuberance. "When I spied you across the way, I thought the same thing. Two years ago, I would have never believed that we'd have the chance to see each other so much."

"And now we live in the same town."

"We are blessed."

Belatedly realizing that she'd ignored Levi completely, she turned to him. "Good day, Levi."

"Tess. Good day to you." His brown eyes were full of humor as he stared at her. "I would ask how you are doing, but I can't imagine you are anything but happy right now. You look like the cat who's gotten all the cream."

She chuckled. "I am happy. Not only did I run into you both, but something wonderful happened this morning."

Simon crossed his arms over his chest. "Well,

don't keep us on pins and needles. What happened?"

"A mother and her son came into The Refuge. They were running away from an abusive boyfriend. The mom trusted me enough to allow me to contact a social worker and a policeman, too. Then, she called a friend who she'd been afraid to reach out to and that girlfriend is going to take them in." She paused, still feeling like what had happened had been so right. "I feel like I made a difference today. That makes me mighty happy."

"Congratulations, Tess," Levi said. "You are right. It's *wunderbaar*."

"And don't forget that all of this is your doing, Tess," Simon said. "You should feel proud."

"I'm just glad I could help them. It's the best feeling." Impulsively, she reached out and hugged him.

After a slight pause, he hugged her back. "Is this going to be a habit?" he teased. "Are you going to start hugging me in the produce aisle?"

"I hope so."

His hazel eyes brightened. "I'm not one for hugging, but I'll try to get used to it."

"Oh, I have a feeling you hug that pretty fiancée of yours from time to time."

Levi groaned. "Oh, don't get him started. If we're not careful, he'll talk about my little sister all day long."

Simon frowned at him. "There ain't a thing wrong with that."

"Of course there isn't," Tess said quickly. She would have never imagined her street-smart, reserved brother would ever be so unabashedly smitten, but it did her heart good. It gave her hope that one day she and Jeremy could be in healthy, happy relationships, too. They certainly deserved some happiness.

And, speaking of relationships and happiness . . . she had a supper to make! "So, what are you two doing here?" she asked.

"Amelia asked me to stop by the store on the way home," Simon said. "She's making buttermilk chicken for supper but ran out of buttermilk."

"Since no one is cooking me supper, I had to get some supplies for myself," Levi said as he held up a basket of bread, lunch meat, and a bag of sliced carrots.

"You should join us," Simon said. "Lukas and Amelia would be pleased to see you."

"*Danke*, but maybe another time."

Simon turned to her. "What are you in here for? I'm thinking you've got a lot of food in your cart for one girl."

"It's actually for me and a friend." Feeling a little embarrassed, she said, "I'm having someone over for supper on Friday night. I decided to get the shopping done ahead of time."

"Who are you having over? Anyone I know?"

To her amusement, Simon was looking concerned and protective. "*Nee*, I don't think so."

"I'm glad you're making some friends already," he said, his expression warm. "I didn't know you'd met any girls."

She didn't want to lie to him. And while again, she didn't owe him anything or want anything from him—not even his approval—she forced herself to tell him the truth. "I've met a couple, but I actually invited a man for supper."

His eyes narrowed. "You have a date? And you're cooking for him, too?"

"*Jah.*"

"Is that safe? Do you know him well?"

"Well enough."

"Are you sure? Having a strange man over at your house seems like a pretty big step. Maybe you should be meeting him at a restaurant." He brightened. "Remember how you liked Josephine's Café? You could meet him there. I could even stop by. If you got uncomfortable, you wouldn't have to worry. Amelia will love eating out on Friday night."

"Definitely not."

"Tess, I really think you should reconsider this. It's better to be safe than sorry, you know."

Oh, but he was being silly. Didn't he remember that she'd been on her own for years? "I don't think I have to be afraid of this man. He's a cop."

Levi raised his eyebrows. "Who is it?"

"Ken Perry. Do you know him?"

"His name sounds familiar." Turning to Simon,

he said, "I'll talk to Lukas and Rebecca. They've always dealt with the office more than I have. The police come in from time to time, you know. Just to make sure everything is okay."

Right as Simon was about to nod, Tess cut him off. "I don't need either of you to check Ken out. Please don't."

Back went Simon's arms across his chest. "Is this the same man you met the other day?"

"He's stopped by The Refuge several times. Today he was the one who came over when that woman and her child showed up. He helped me get her assistance, Simon. He knows about my past, too. He's a nice man."

"Huh."

She rolled her eyes. "Simon, enough. You are acting like I need someone to watch out for me. I don't."

"Everyone does."

"How about this, then. What would you have thought about me questioning everything about you and Amelia?"

He looked so shocked, she almost laughed. "You wouldn't have liked me interfering one bit."

"You wouldn't have needed to wonder about me and Amelia, Tess."

"Why, because you are a man and I'm a woman?"

"*Nee.* Because Amelia Kinsinger is pretty much perfect."

She opened her mouth, closed it again, then felt her heart warm. Amelia was sweet and lovely inside and out. But what Tess had really liked about her was that she didn't let Simon walk all over her. She gave him his way but held her ground when they didn't agree.

"You're right," she said with a small smile. "Amelia is pretty much perfect. At least, she seems perfect for you."

"She is. I cannot wait to marry her."

"You sound anxious."

"You don't even know. I've waited years for her to be mine."

Levi grunted. "That's my little sister. Don't be talking about longing for her around me, if you please."

Tess giggled. "I think that's our cue to get back to our shopping."

"I'll come over soon to see how the date went," Simon said.

"Come over anytime, *bruder*," she said in Pennsylvania Dutch. "Anytime I see you is the best time. That is, anytime except Friday night."

She couldn't help but grin when he scowled at her.

Chapter 13

❄ ❄ ❄

December 7, Evening

"Huh. So, this is it," Lukas said as he walked through the front door to Levi's house. He stood still, an expression of distaste on his face as Darla, Amelia, Simon, Rebecca, and Jacob filled the rest of his small entryway.

As Levi closed the door, he realized that he'd probably never heard his siblings be this quiet. "Yep, this is it," he repeated with more than a little bit of false enthusiasm in his tone.

"It's cleaner than I imagined," Amelia said with a small smile. "And warm, too. That's *gut*."

Simon helped Amelia remove her cloak before setting it on one of the hooks by the front door. "It is warm." After he pulled off his coat, he pulled at the sleeves of his white shirt. "Maybe too warm."

"The fireplace works well," Levi explained. "It's one of the best things about the place."

"I bet," Rebecca said. Her tone of voice hinted that she thought the working fireplace was the only positive thing to be found.

"Take off your coats, everyone. Make yourself at home."

Almost in unison, the others did as he bid and took off their cloaks and jackets. Because the entryway was so small and there were only three hooks, most of them placed their coats over the back of his couch.

Then, they all simply stood and looked around.

The silence and tension was making Levi feel even more uneasy. "Why are you all so quiet?" he teased. "Usually, all of you have more than enough to say about things."

"I think we're trying to be kind," Rebecca finally said. "You know what Mamm used to say. If you can't think of anything nice, don't say anything at all."

Amelia frowned. "I don't think that was too nice, Becky."

"I'm trying, though."

Levi grinned. "Don't hold your tongue on my account, Rebecca. I can take whatever you have to say."

But instead of taking his bait, she stepped a little closer to her husband, almost as if she needed Jacob for support. "It ain't that, Levi. I, well, I simply don't know what to say about this place of yours. It practically leaves me speechless."

"Oh, come on. It ain't that bad."

Lukas grunted. "Sure it is," he said. "It's tiny and dingy."

"It smells, too," Jacob added. "No offense, but someone with a powerful penchant for cigarettes smoked in here. A lot."

"It does smell," Darla said. "So much that it kind of makes one wonder if your smokers ever left."

Even though he hated the musty scent, too, Levi felt himself getting defensive. "The smell isn't that strong."

Amelia bit her lip. "I fear it is, Levi."

"Would you all like some *kaffi*? I made a fresh pot right before you arrived."

"Was your percolator clean?" Rebecca asked, her voice full of unwelcome skepticism.

"It is. It's as clean as yours. Maybe cleaner. It's brand-new."

Lukas cleared his throat as he sat down in the easy chair. "*Kaffi* sounds great. *Danke*."

"I'll help you," Amelia said.

"*Nee*, Amy," Simon said. "You go sit down, I'll help your brother."

Noticing that the others gingerly sat down, too, Levi felt every muscle in his neck knot up.

Once they got into his kitchen, he glared at Simon. "Do you not trust Amelia to help in my kitchen?"

"Of course I trust her. But I try to look after her when I can. She works at the family home all day, you know. She makes supper, breakfast, looks after the animals, and does all the laundry.

I hate to see her wait on people when she is away from home."

Simon had sounded bitter. Levi wondered why. As he poured coffee into seven mugs, all which happened to be new, too, he said, "Amelia working so hard at the house ain't my fault. You know she likes taking care of the home."

"Oh, I know."

"Grab the milk and sugar," Levi ordered, then lowered his voice. "Then why do you sound so put out by it? She'll be doing the same thing for you when she's your wife, right?"

"My place isn't as big as your family's farmhouse. We know that."

"Then what's the problem?"

"Maybe the fact that you have a nice house, a really nice house that has been in your family for generations. You've got a sister there doing her best to make it a home for you."

"And?"

"And you threw it all away." He waved a hand. "For this."

Picking up two of the mugs, Levi sighed. How was he even going to be able to explain to them that he hadn't thrown anything away at all? He'd simply been too weak to handle being home without hearing his father's voice echo down the hall.

He wasn't sure he'd ever be able to confess so much.

Because of that, he said, "I don't want to argue with you. Let's go join everyone."

"Probably a good idea."

After they delivered all the mugs, Levi sat down on the floor in front of the fireplace.

"The coffee is good," Darla said.

She definitely sounded surprised. "*Danke*," he replied, not even trying to hide the amusement in his voice. "I've, ah, had a lot of experience making coffee. Do you all want a tour?"

"Maybe in a little while," she answered after looking at Lukas.

Levi was becoming annoyed. "What has you all acting like this? You wanted to come here and see it. What's more, I've never been shy about describing the state it's in."

"You don't want me to say what's on my mind," Lukas said.

"*Nee*, I actually do. You all are acting like you're embarrassed that I'm living here."

Lukas waved a hand. "That's not it at all."

"Then what is it?"

"This . . . this place is fine. I don't have a problem with Jupiter Street at all. You know as well I do that many of our friends and workers live here. I've visited many of them at their houses from time to time with Daed over the years."

"Then?"

"What I can't seem to get my mind around is the fact that you should not be here in the first place."

"That, and it smells and needs fresh paint," Rebecca said.

Looking at Simon, Levi said, "First of all, I'm not here because I don't appreciate our house or our family."

"Then why?"

"I just wanted a little bit of space," he lied. "When the lease is up, I'll go home. After that, I'll sit down with Lukas and Darla and figure out what I should do next."

His brother frowned. "Next? What do you mean, next?"

Because he still didn't want to admit how hard it was to live in that house without either parent, he sidestepped the question. "Lukas, the house is yours. You and Darla live there."

"There's room for more than two people, Levi," Darla said.

"True, but it ain't a place for two married brothers to live."

"Do you have plans to get married soon?"

"You know what I mean, Becky. One day I'll be like the rest of you and be getting married."

"I don't understand why that would be a problem," Amelia said.

"It's not a problem. It simply means I'll need to find a different place to live."

Lukas shook his head. "No, it doesn't. The house is as much yours or Amelia's or Rebecca's as it is mine."

Because it was tradition for the house to be passed on to the oldest son, he said, "Lukas, you are the oldest. You and Darla will need the space. It should go to you."

"Our house is sprawling and huge, Levi. There are six bedrooms and five bathrooms. There's even the small kitchen nook that Daed built years ago when our grandparents were still living. I don't see any reason why we couldn't share the house."

They had talked him into a corner. He'd tried to give them multiple, meaningless excuses to explain his complex feelings.

Just as he was about to say that newly married couples needed privacy, he thought of Julia. She'd lost a husband, moved to a new town, and was raising a little girl without complaint. If she could rebound so well after a devastating death, he needed to be honest with both himself and his siblings.

Taking a deep breath, he said, "I can hardly stand to be in the house." There. He'd said it. Feeling embarrassment wash over him, he waited for the questions to come.

A couple of seconds passed.

A couple more.

Then Rebecca asked the question that no doubt all of them were thinking. "Why?"

Gazing at the wall so he wouldn't have to face them, he said, "It has too many memories. It hurts. I . . . well, I keep listening for Daed's voice. I keep remembering how Mamm would fuss at us for not picking up our clothes off the floor."

"Or not washing our hands good enough," Rebecca murmured. "Mamm loved to examine our hands and nails."

"I remember Mamm laughing on her birthdays," Amelia whispered. "Daed always made her a cake."

"*Nee*, he always tried to make her a cake," Lukas said, sounding hoarse. "It never turned out. Mamm would laugh and eat her piece, though." He paused. "When she died, Daed never made another birthday cake."

Amelia wiped her eyes. "Sometimes, when we are all together, I keep looking at the door, waiting for Daed to come in."

Levi felt himself get choked up. If he wasn't careful, he was going to start crying. But just as he tried to hide his weakness yet again, he looked at his siblings.

Really looked at them.

Lukas was clutching Darla's hand. Rebecca was biting her bottom lip, and Amelia—sweet Amelia —wasn't even trying to stop the flow of her tears. Simon handed her a worn handkerchief.

"You all are still grieving, too," he said. "I'm not the only one who is having a hard time."

Lukas shook his head. "I still wake up in the middle of the night, sure I smell smoke. And then

I sit and wonder why I didn't do more to save Daed."

"You couldn't have saved him," Levi said.

"I know, but that doesn't seem to matter at two in the morning. What does matter is that you aren't alone, Levi. I still have difficult days."

"We all do," Rebecca said. "I'm sorry you thought you had to hide your feelings."

He couldn't believe how much lighter he felt. "I should have been more honest." Turning to Darla, he said, "I was angry and sad and embarrassed that I wasn't as strong as the rest of my family. I should never have blamed your father for the accident. I really never should have taken my hurt out on you."

Darla walked over and hugged Levi tightly. "It's over. It's all over with now. Let's stop apologizing and move forward."

When she released him and went back to Lukas's side, he said, "I'll try my best to move forward."

"You don't need to do anything but be yourself," Lukas said. "That's all I want. Move home soon and be with us again."

Looking at the people he loved most in the world, Levi felt hopeful for the first time in almost a year. "Do you think it really could work?"

"Of course it can," said Amelia with a teary smile.

"I do think it can work," Lukas said. "After all, it's not like we aren't used to appreciating each other's boundaries. Then, there's the fact that we've lived most of our lives in the same house. At the very least, we could give it a try."

Lukas's chin lifted. "So, will you come back home?"

"I'd like to move back home." Thinking of Julia and Penny, he added, "But first, I need to see how some other things go in my life."

"What things?" Rebecca asked.

"Maybe Julia and her daughter?" Amelia asked hopefully.

"*Nee* . . ." When the whole crowd of them stared back with various stages of disbelief, Levi rolled his eyes. "Okay, maybe I am."

As was her way, Rebecca clapped her hands. "This is wonderful. Do you really think she might be the woman for you?"

"Maybe. I hope so. I know I want to get to know her better."

Jacob shifted slightly. "I don't want to sound mean, but are you worried about her having been married before? That she had a child from a previous marriage?"

"I think her experiences can only help us both. Since she's been married before, she'll likely know how we're supposed to handle things. I have no idea."

Lukas grinned. "You might have a point there.

But of course, you shouldn't forget that you have all of us. We've all begun successful relationships and would be glad to share our newfound knowledge." Looking at Darla, he winked. "For the record, I happen to be great at marriage."

"I'll keep that in mind," Levi said and also winked at Darla.

Simon grinned. "You thinking of entering matrimony, Levi? Do you need some advice about going courting?"

"Not from you." Tired of talking about himself, Levi got to his feet. "I'm thinking that this conversation has run its course. Now, how about a tour?"

"Yes, let's have a tour. I, for one, can't wait to see what you've done with the place," Rebecca said.

"Sarcasm doesn't favor you, sister," Levi blurted.

"Neither does this place, brother," she replied, matching his tone word for word. "Now lead on so we can get this tour over with."

Chapter 14

❄ ❄ ❄

Friday Night, December 9

It wasn't supposed to be like this. By the time she'd reached thirty-five, Tess had assumed that she would have had this dating thing down pat. Actually, she'd always assumed that she would have been happily married by the time she was in her early thirties, not starting over in a new job, a new town, and cooking dinner for a man she didn't know very well.

However, here she was, overcome by doubts and nervousness and questioning everything about this date, from the simple meal of chili to the way she'd set the table, to what she was wearing.

Her fourth outfit.

As she gazed at herself in the mirror, turning this way and that, Tess pressed both palms on her stomach in a puny effort to control her butterflies.

It didn't help.

Nope, she didn't feel any more confident or self-assured than she had two minutes ago. If anything, she was only plagued by more doubts . . . and was seriously regretting making spicy chili for Ken.

But since it was currently simmering on the

stove, she forced herself to examine her reflection. She looked okay. Kind of.

But . . . maybe she shouldn't have decided on her best red cashmere sweater? She'd put it on because she'd thought it looked festive, but it probably looked like she was trying too hard.

She pulled at the expensive knit. Plus, it was looking a bit too snug. Frowning, Tess sucked in her stomach. She really needed to stop eating so much Amish food. From now on, only salads, and not Amish potato salad, either.

Then there was her hair. She'd just got it cut. But now the blunt, choppy cut that grazed her shoulders looked out of place instead of current. What would Ken think? Maybe she needed to start growing it out again.

She was just about to analyze the way her jeans fit when the doorbell rang.

Glad to have temporarily gotten out of that nightmare, Tess practically scampered down the stairs and rushed across the entryway to open the door.

And there was Ken standing on the other side. Holding a bouquet of flowers.

Flowers!

He was wearing jeans, too. But he also had on a white button-down, an expensive-looking leather belt, boots, and a dark-navy blazer. He looked handsome. Really handsome, and so different than when he was in his uniform.

"Hi," she said, feeling awkward all over again. Maybe she should have put on a dress.

"Hi back," he said. As he studied her, the corners of his lips curved up. "Can I come in?"

Abruptly, she stepped backward on her three-inch heels. "Of course. Come in." Feeling her cheeks heat, she cleared her throat. "I mean, Ken, welcome. Please come in."

His hint of a smile morphed into a full-fledged grin. "Uh-oh," he said.

Her eyes widened. "What?"

"You look like you're biting your tongue, and that means I no doubt did something stupid. I'm trying to decide if I'm too early, too overdressed, or tried too hard by bringing you flowers. Which is it?"

She was so surprised, she grinned, too. "You haven't done anything wrong."

He tilted his head to one side. "Are you sure?"

"Very sure. I . . . well, I guess I'm a little nervous." Sheepishly she added, "I've actually been upstairs trying on outfits for the last half hour."

New appreciation lit his eyes. "I'm no fashion expert, but I think you did a good job. I like your red sweater. The heels, too."

"*Danke.* I mean, thank you." She held out her hands. "Would you like me to take your coat?"

"I'll keep my blazer on for now." When she simply stood there, he gestured toward the kitchen. "Maybe we could put these flowers in water?"

"Hmm? Oh, yes. That's a good idea." Taking the bouquet from him, she noticed that there were red roses and carnations, baby's breath and pretty greenery, too. "This is so Christmasy. It's really pretty."

"I liked it. I'm glad you like it, too."

"I do." Belatedly, she realized that she hadn't even thanked him yet. "Thank you for the flowers," she said as they entered the kitchen. "No one's ever given me flowers before."

"Really? I'm surprised."

"You shouldn't be." Kneeling down, she reached for a water pitcher. "Do you think this will do? I don't have a vase."

"I think it will do just fine," he said softly.

Tess didn't have a lot of experience with dating, but she had a feeling that getting flowers at the beginning of it meant they were off to a great start.

After she unwrapped the flowers from the butcher paper they'd been carefully wrapped in, she took her time arranging the flowers in the plastic water pitcher. When she was done, she held it up. "What do you think?"

"They look beautiful." Holding out his hands, he said, "How about I put them on the table?"

"That would be great." She smiled awkwardly again. Then, the moment his back was turned, she took a revitalizing breath. He was dressed up, smiling at her, and had brought her flowers.

He'd been as eager for this date as she had been!

At last, she started feeling better about herself. "I wanted our corn bread to be warm, so I decided to wait until you were here to put it in the oven." After she put the muffin pan into the oven, she asked, "Would you like something to drink while it bakes? I have pop and water and beer." She didn't drink, but she'd thought maybe a man like him might want a beer or something.

"A Coke would be great. Thanks."

By the time she followed him into the small living room, two glasses of pop in her hands, Tess was starting to think that she was getting the hang of this dating thing after all.

"Here you go," she said as she set his glass on the table.

"Thanks," he replied before looking down at his boots, and grinning. "Do you think we're ever going to relax tonight?"

"We? Are you nervous, too?"

"Oh, yeah." He rolled his eyes. "You may not get all that many bouquets of flowers, but you're the first woman I've ever bought any for."

She sat down on the couch. "Really? Why me, then? I mean, if you don't mind me asking."

He shrugged as he joined her on the couch. "Because I didn't want to mess this up." He chuckled under his breath. "I don't want to scare you or anything, but, well, before you asked me over for dinner, I was trying to get the nerve to ask you out again."

Ken was just telling her that he cared enough about her to be trying so hard. He didn't know it, but after the life she'd had, nothing could mean more to her.

"I'm not scared," she finally said.

"If this dinner goes okay, maybe I could take you out on a real date real soon? You know, the kind where I pick you up and take you out to a restaurant? My brothers told me I shouldn't have made you cook for me on a first date."

His honesty made her chuckle again. "Since I don't know what I'm doing either, I don't mind that we're here instead of out in public. I'd probably spill my water glass or knock over someone's table. Now, at least, I'll only embarrass myself in front of you."

"So far, you haven't spilled anything and the table is still right side up. I guess that means you're doing great."

Tess giggled as the last of her doubts dissipated. Wanting to set him at ease, she said, "You aren't the only one who got on the phone to get advice. I actually called Jill, my foster mom, a couple of hours ago."

"She give you any words of wisdom?"

"Nothing out of the ordinary . . . though she did say if you had fun and wanted to see me again you would call me tomorrow or something. I think that means you're supposed to wait until one date is over before asking me out on another one."

"Probably. But since I've already messed that up, would you put me out of my misery now?"

"Your misery?"

"May I take you out soon?"

"Yes," she whispered. "I think I'd like that a lot."

He grinned. "Now that we got that out of the way, want to hear about what happened on traffic duty yesterday? It involves a horse and buggy, two teenagers on bikes, and a truck filled with Christmas trees."

Leaning back, she smiled at him. "Tell me everything, and don't skimp on the details."

Then she leaned back and simply enjoyed being with him.

Chapter 15

❄ ❄ ❄

Saturday, December 10

On Saturday afternoon, when Levi opened his door to see Julia with Penny at her side, he once again felt like he'd received a sweet gift.

There was just something about Julia that appealed to him. Today, she had on a dark forest-green dress. The color set off her golden hair, light-brown eyes, and creamy skin. When she smiled at him and he caught sight of her dimple, he felt like a foolish teenaged boy, a little flustered, a little tongue-tied.

"Hey, you two," he said, hoping he sounded a whole lot more composed than he felt. "This is a nice surprise."

Julia's smile faded as her expression turned a little more unsure. "I hope we didn't interrupt anything?"

"Not at all. I was just, um, reading the paper." What he'd actually been doing was staring out the window and thinking about his father and missing him, but there was no way he was going to admit that. He hated admitting to anyone that he was still having a difficult time. "Come on in."

Still, she hesitated. Pointing to her tote bag, she said, "I only had to work a few hours this morning, so Penny and I were hoping that we could finish cleaning your *haus* this afternoon. Would you mind if we came in? I promise, we won't bother you none."

The absolute last thing he wanted was to sit in his ugly living room and listen to Julia clean his bathroom. "Julia, there's no need."

"I'm afraid there is. Your home needs a good cleaning, Levi." Smiling softly at her daughter, who was clutching a worn teddy bear, Julia continued softly. "Penny and I won't be any trouble. She's going to sit with me while I work."

"I can't let you do that. There's no way I can stand to one side while you are scrubbing my floors and poor Penny is sitting there watching you. I'll feel terrible. That's no way to spend a Saturday afternoon."

But instead of looking reassured, she nibbled her bottom lip. "I'd rather not come over tomorrow, that's the Lord's day. And I'm afraid Monday is a workday for me."

"That's okay. You don't have to come back to clean."

But instead of looking relieved, she looked rather put out. And, perhaps, a little panicked? "Levi, please—" She stopped herself and turned to Penny. "Penny, dear, go sit down on Levi's couch for a moment, wouldja? I need to speak to

Mr. Levi about something that's just for grown-up ears."

Penny looked at him apprehensively, shifting from one foot to the other. "Mommy, I don't think Mr. Levi wants me to do that."

Great. Now he was frightening a child. "I don't mind at all, Penny," he said gently. "You go sit down with your bear, okay? Anywhere is fine."

Penny trotted over to the couch, looking back at her mother nervously as she did so.

Once her little girl was out of earshot, Julia stepped a bit closer. "Did I do something wrong?" she whispered.

"*Nee.* Of course not."

"Well then, do ya remember what I said about the present I was hoping to buy? Christmas is coming and I still haven't been able to afford it yet. I'm sorry, but I thought you were serious about your needing me to clean your home. I was counting on that money."

Of course. Because Christmas was on the way.

Hating the thought of her working so hard for an amount of money he wouldn't really miss, he said, "How about you let me simply help you with the gift?"

When she stared at him in confusion, he explained. "I can lend you the money, Julia. Actually, I'd be happy to do that."

Her expression hardened. "You'll do no such thing. I don't want your charity."

"It wasn't charity. I was thinking it could be more of a gift between friends." Of course, the moment he heard his words, he ached to take them back. He sounded so eager. And, maybe, more than a little presumptuous. Did she even think of the two of them as friends?

"I would appreciate the gift, but I'd much rather you let me have my way instead."

He noticed her eyes were sparkling now. He really did like how Julia had a bit of spunk and fire in her. She might be a woman with her fair share of struggles, but she was certainly no pushover.

He was going to need to let her have her way. "All right. How about this? How about I help you clean and then we do something fun?"

She stopped in mid-nod. "That isn't necessary."

This woman. This Julia. Every new facet that he was learning about her made him smile. She was so tough, yet he was sure her shell covered a soft, tender girl underneath. She was so different than almost any woman he'd ever met. Maybe it was because she was a widow. Maybe it was even because she was a little older than him. Whatever the reason, he was intrigued by her many layers. So intrigued, he was even willing to do whatever it took to get to know her a whole lot better.

Why, he'd even clean his house in order to spend time with her.

"Please?" he asked.

She looked dumbstruck. " 'Please'?"

"Yeah. I . . . Julia, you know what I'm saying, right? I want to spend time with you and Penny today."

"Can we, Mommy?" Penny asked from the couch.

Julia closed her eyes as a blush floated across her face. "I guess we forgot to keep our voices down."

"Well, we can't disappoint her, can we?" He smiled then. His best smile, the one he used to pull out at school or on his mother when he really wanted something.

Julia looked up at him, her light-brown eyes looking almost golden in the morning sun. Her expression softened as she looked at her daughter. At last, she nodded. "All right. I suppose we could do that."

Levi grinned as he felt some of the air he'd been holding in his lungs slowly filter out. He'd been that worried she'd refuse him!

He turned and looked down the hall. "Where should we clean first?"

"I . . . well, I was thinking we could tackle your bedroom today. I was going to change the sheets, sweep, and dust, too."

It was going to feel a little odd, the three of them in his bedroom, but just as quickly, he shook off his apprehension as a foolish thought. It was just a room in his house and she was right. It was rather dusty. "Let's get to it, then." Raising his voice a bit, he said, "Penny, do you want to come sit with us while we clean my room?"

Penny trotted off the couch and hurried to his side. "*Jah.*"

Seeing that Julia had already walked ahead, he looked down at Penny. "You are surely one of the sweetest girls I've ever met. Not too many kids I know would sit with their mothers while they cleaned."

Penny looked up at him with solemn eyes. "I sat with Mommy all the time when we lived at the motel. She makes beds better than anyone. Everyone there said so."

"I can't wait to see my bed, then. That will be quite a treat."

She tilted her head to one side. "A treat? Why?"

"Because I don't think I've made my bed in weeks."

"Mr. Levi, that ain't *gut*."

He laughed. "I think you're right about that," he said as they walked into the bedroom. Julia had already stripped all the sheets from the bed and was on her hands and knees using a rag or a mop of some sort to clean the wood floor underneath it.

Immediately, he knelt down beside her. "What can I do?"

She looked startled to see him there, but she recovered quickly. "Pick up your bedding and take it downstairs, then bring me my tote bag.

We've got a lot of work to do to make this space shine, Mr. Kinsinger."

He stood up and grabbed the bedding, meeting Penny's gaze as he did so.

She smirked from where she now sat, cross-legged against the wall. "I told ya. *Mei mommi*'s a real *gut* cleaner."

As he walked down the hall, his arms filled with sheets and blankets, Levi decided Julia Kemp was a whole lot more than that. Far more.

Chapter 16

❄ ❄ ❄

As Julia wiped her brow while she walked down the short hallway to join Levi and Penny in his sparse family room, she knew she needed to face facts. First, Levi was keeping her company because he needed to get his house in order. It was a mess, too.

A real mess. Actually, his housekeeping skills had a lot to be desired.

Because of all that, he was paying her to clean. That was why she was there.

Once she came to terms with that, she definitely needed to remember to never, ever, ask him to help her clean anything ever again.

He was worse than a two-year-old. He got off track. He talked instead of dusting. He kept teasing Penny, which meant that he would sit with her little girl and giggle and play when he should have kept his mind on their task at hand.

But worse than even all of those was that Levi was completely, hopelessly, irresistible to her.

He was so different than most of the men she'd ever been around. Her father was a kind sort of person, but he was quiet and a bit reserved. Other men she'd known believed in men's and women's roles in life. They would have never sat with her while she cleaned.

Levi was kind and fun. Flirty and humorous. Somehow he'd even made her laugh while she'd been cleaning the corners of his closet!

She liked his carefree attitude. She liked the way he doted on her daughter. She liked his warm gazes and his slow smiles.

She liked it all so much that she would even sometimes find herself forgetting that she was there to do a job. That she was only there in order to buy a Christmas gift for Penny.

And that, of course, meant that she was liking Levi's company far too much.

"Julia, are you ever going to come in here to play cards with us?" Levi called out. "Penny and I have been waiting ever so patiently."

"*I've* been waiting patiently, Mommy," Penny corrected. "Mr. Levi hasn't been patient at all."

"I'm here now," she said as she set her tote bag down by the door. When she noticed the paper with a dozen games of tic-tac-toe scribbled on it, the pile of cards from a fallen card house, and a pile of pretzel crumbs, she shook her head in wonder. "I don't think either of you have been waiting patiently."

"We tried," Penny protested, looking at Levi for reassurance.

He nodded. “We did. But we got hungry.”

“And we weren’t too good at building card towers.”

“And we would rather be playing Go Fish instead of dusting.”

Julia eyed the stack of cards meaningfully. “Or picking up after yourselves?”

Levi laughed. “I’m a mess, I admit it.”

“I must agree with you there.” She sat on the floor next to them. “However, you will appreciate your hard work when you crawl in between your fresh, sweet-smelling sheets tonight, Mr. Levi.”

Looking a bit more reflective, he nodded. “You are right about that. I will be feeling thankful tonight for many reasons. For sure and for cer-tain.”

There went the butterflies again. They were dancing around in her stomach, practically doing somersaults every time he smiled at her.

He was so smooth. His words so glib. She shouldn’t be affected by them. But she was. He was awakening something inside of her that she’d been certain had become a memory.

“Well, what are we waiting for?” she teased. “Let’s play Go Fish.”

“Can we have hot chocolate now, too?” Penny asked. “And maybe a fire because it’s snowy out and cold?”

“I doubt Mr. Levi has—”

“I do,” Levi interrupted. “But if we have those

two things, we're going to need popcorn, too. What do you think, Pen? Shall we pop some popcorn?"

Penny was staring at him like he'd just told her that he could lasso the moon. "We can have that, too?"

"Of course we can. You, Miss Penny, are too easy to please." Getting to his feet, he held out a hand. "Come on, let's make popcorn and hot chocolate while your mother rests for a moment."

She felt silly, sprawled out on the floor while Levi and Penny stood above her. "I'll get up, too. I don't need to rest."

"Maybe you don't. But I would like to see you sit and relax for a change. I don't think you do that very often."

She didn't. She hadn't. She was about to protest that it wasn't a mother's place to sit and rest while others worked, but she couldn't find the willpower to do that. She was enjoying the sight of Penny's happiness too much.

Levi bent down to help her up. "Go sit on my couch, Julia. Please."

Please. There was that word again. And just like before, it made her skin break out in goose bumps. One tiny word meant so much to her. He didn't know it, but he could probably convince her to do just about anything with that word.

She got to her feet and sank into the sofa, adjusting her body so she could watch the flames in the fireplace. Then she allowed herself to simply sit and listen to Levi and Penny open and shut cabinets and fill his kettle with water.

Levi sounded extremely content as he directed little Penny around his kitchen, helping her climb onto a small stepstool in order to retrieve mugs from cabinets and popcorn kernels from a different spot.

Julia didn't need to see Penny to know how happy she was. Her voice was merry as she asked Levi about his hot chocolate mix and whether or not he liked bunnies and goats.

"Bunnies and goats?" he cried out. "What got you thinking about them?"

" 'Cause they have them at Hershberger's. Have you been there?"

"Once or twice."

"Well, they have baby bunnies and goats in the spring. I mean, I heard they do. Gretel told me about that."

"Gretel told you? Would that Gretel happen to be Gretel Kurtz, my sister-in-law Darla's little sister?"

"I'm not sure."

"If she is, I know she'll be a good friend for you. She's a nice girl. Kind."

"Oh, we already are friends, Mr. Levi," Penny said with a giggle. "We play on the monkey bars all the time."

As Levi teased Penny about climbing on monkey

bars, Julia felt her insides take a little tumble all over again.

For most of Penny's life, it had always just been the two of them. She hadn't had a lot of opportunities to play with other children.

She also hadn't been around too many adults who took the time to chat with her. While Connie and Jared were kind and helped her tremendously, they were also her bosses. Julia never forgot that they were responsible for her having a place to live and a way to support herself and her daughter. Because of that, she always made sure that Penny was on her best behavior around them.

Connie and Jared were also Mennonite. And while that didn't mean that they didn't have anything in common in regards to their religion, it also was an added barrier to fostering a close friendship.

Now things were so different.

Now Penny was in school and was making friends of her own. And now they lived in a house and were meeting other people on equal terms. Instead of being known as one of the motel's maids, now Julia thought of herself as a mother in the community, a mother just like so many other moms in the area. It was a big difference of how others perceived her.

But the biggest difference in both of their lives was Levi Kinsinger. He made them both feel like they were special.

"Here we are, Mommy!" Penny called out as she led the way into the living room. "We've got hot chocolate and popcorn, and you didn't even have to help make it."

Eyes shining, Levi smiled at her. "She's right. When was the last time that someone brought you hot chocolate and popcorn?"

"That's not hard to answer. Not in at least eight or ten years, I reckon."

Levi stared at her. "It's been that long?"

For some reason, she felt a little embarrassed. "I'm a grown woman, Levi," she pointed out. "Grown women don't sit around and wait to be served."

"I know that. But did your husband never fuss over you?"

"*Nee*, he did not." When Penny's eyes widened, Julia realized that her voice had probably turned hoarse.

No doubt because she hated the web of lies that she seemed to be continually heaping onto her past, one right after the other. "That, um, that wasn't his way."

Levi studied her another moment before grinning at Penny. "If your mother has been so sorely neglected, I think we're going to need to take mighty good care of her from now on. Ain't so?"

Penny nodded as she knelt on the ground and pushed the thick stoneware bowl across the coffee table and then sat next to her mother. "Here, Mommy. You can have the first bite."

After popping a couple of the fluffy white pieces into her mouth, she raised her eyebrows. "Do you both mean to tell me that you didn't sneak any pieces at all?"

Levi and Penny shared a guilty glance. Julia thought their exchange was adorable.

"Maybe one," Levi said with a wink at Penny.

"Maybe more than one," Penny said with another giggle. Glancing at Julia again, she pulled in her bottom lip. "Does it matter, Mommy?"

At last, she was able to answer without a single hesitation—or fib. "It doesn't matter at all. Not one bit."

Picking up the deck of cards, Levi said, "I think it's time for us to stop talking and play cards."

Holding out her hands, Julia nodded. "I think so, too. Since you all made the popcorn, I'll shuffle."

When Levi handed her the cards and their fingertips brushed, she felt his gaze warm on her. When they exchanged a glance, she smiled softly.

She hadn't been so happy in a mighty long time. It was a good feeling. Truly, a lovely one.

One that she'd never take for granted ever again.

Chapter 17

❄ ❄ ❄

Friday, December 16

"Penny, I know this is uncomfortable, but keep this under your tongue another minute," Julia murmured as she slipped the thermometer under her daughter's tongue.

Penny grimaced but didn't fight her like she had the day before. Now, instead of squirming and fussing, she lay listlessly in Julia's arms, her eyes at half-mast, her flushed skin looking papery and dry.

Julia kept her eyes on her daughter's, ruthlessly trying to look optimistic even though everything inside of her told her that things with Penny were worse. Much worse.

When the thermometer beeped, Julia slid it out of Penny's mouth in relief. Then she could barely stifle a gasp when she read the reading. 104.3. It was too high.

Yesterday it had hovered around 103 and Penny had been whiny and fretful. She'd complained about her ears hurting and whined about her throat burning something awful. She hadn't wanted to listen to any of the books Julia tried to read aloud, and only wanted to sip ginger ale.

Julia had been diligently giving her the children's pain reliever, but the recommended dosage hadn't seemed to make much of a difference in how her little girl felt. Her fever had raged on and she'd cried intermittently until she'd fallen into a fitful sleep.

Now she didn't seem to be interested in anything. Not ginger ale, not her storybooks, not Christmas, not anything. Worse, her eyes looked glassy and she seemed to only want to sleep. Julia didn't need to hear a doctor say that Penny needed to get medical help as soon as possible.

Julia was going to have to take her to the clinic. On a normal day, it would be a nerve-wracking experience. It involved a bike ride or necessitated her borrowing one of her neighbors' horses and buggies.

But now, with the weather so snowy and cold, the idea of driving an unfamiliar buggy and horse in those conditions was terrifying.

But she had no choice.

After settling Penny back in bed, Julia pulled up the covers to her chin and then sat on the side. "Penny, I'm going to have to go borrow someone's horse and buggy so I can take ya to the clinic. I hate to leave you alone, but I'll be back as soon as I can. Okay?"

"Okay, Mommy," she said before her eyes drifted closed again.

Quickly, Julia went to her room and pulled on her thickest tights and a cozy forest-green sweater over her dark-navy dress. Then, after putting on her cloak and red gloves, she stood on the front porch and tried to think who might be home at ten in the morning.

Most of her neighbors worked. However, there was an Amish mother with a young baby two houses down from Levi. Julia didn't know Jane Shelton well, but their passing conversations had been friendly.

Her friendliness, combined with the fact that she was another mother, too, seemed like the best choice to seek help from. Surely, another mother would understand how Julia felt.

Feeling a bit better, now that she'd made her decision, Julia crossed the street as quickly as she dared in her thick snow boots. No one had been by to plow since the night before, and the street was covered with at least three or four inches of drifting snow. She hoped the woman's horse didn't mind pulling buggies in the thick slush.

Just as she was walking past Levi's house, he opened his front door. "Julia, what are you doing?" he called out.

She was so surprised to see him, she drew to a stop. "It's midmorning. What are you doing home?"

Instead of answering, he stared at her intently. "I think the question should be what has brought you out in this weather. The temperature is still in the teens."

Before she could explain what she was doing, the barrage of questions continued as he walked down his driveway. "Where's Penny? I heard that school was closed for the day."

"Um, well—"

He frowned and interrupted her again. "And why are you dressed like that? You need a bonnet or a scarf on over your *kapp*, Julia. You're going to catch your death if you aren't careful."

She was too worried to point out that he was currently standing on his driveway in boots that weren't laced and shirtsleeves.

Actually, she was too worried to do anything but tell him the truth. "I'm out here because Penny's sick."

Immediately, concern filled his gaze. "What's wrong?"

"She has a terrible fever. I've got to get her to the clinic as soon as possible."

"If that's so, why are you walking down the street?"

"I don't have a horse. I'm going to see if I can borrow your neighbor's horse and buggy. I've noticed that the Sheltons don't usually use their buggy during the day."

"Hold on a second and I'll go with you," he said as he turned back and went toward his front door. She was too rattled to refuse his offer.

Instead, she simply stood there in the street and prayed that Jane would be home.

When he came back out in less than five minutes, this time with a black knit hat on his head, a black wool coat, and thick, heavy-soled boots that looked like they could walk through anything with ease, she smiled in relief. "*Danke* for coming out. Maybe she won't refuse me if you are here, too."

"I wish you would have come to get me first. Has Penny been sick long?"

"She spiked a fever yesterday and it's been climbing steadily, even though I've been giving her children's pain reliever."

"How high is it?"

"One-hundred four."

He pressed his lips together. "Poor thing." They avoided the sidewalk and went back to the street to walk. He walked by her side and gripped her arm so she wouldn't fall. "I'm sure Jane will let you borrow her buggy."

"I hope so." Suddenly, she started thinking about just how bad the roads were. "But she might not want me to use it. Some horses don't like walking in snow, you know."

"Most horses like it fine."

"What if she's not home or she doesn't want me to borrow it? Then what should I do?"

"One thing at a time, okay? We'll worry about that when we need to." As they walked up the neighbor's recently shoveled driveway, he smiled at her. "I'm so glad I hadn't gone into work yet. I hate the idea of you venturing out in this weather alone."

"How come you are home? You aren't usually."

"It's a long story."

"Is it something bad?"

"Not at all. Only that the weather has messed up a lot of our scheduled deliveries. The driver I was waiting for is running about five hours late."

"Five hours is a long time."

"Tell me about it. I told my crew to come in late. I had been intending to sand the window-sills and apply a fresh coat of paint. But I haven't been doing too much besides staring out the window and watching it snow."

Something in her insides softened at the thought of him enjoying such a simple thing. "Maybe I should be feeling sorry for interrupting your relaxing morning, but I can't feel anything but grateful."

"I'm glad I was here." As they walked up Jane's walkway, also neatly shoveled, he said, "Just last night, I was feeling a bit bothered about today's schedule. I didn't want to have to ask men to come in late and work long hours so close to Christmas. But now I know that the Lord had a plan," he said as he knocked on his neighbor's door.

Jane opened the door with a toddler in one of

her arms. She looked surprised to see them. She smiled hesitantly, shifting her little girl onto one hip. "Yes, Levi? And you are Julia, right?"

"I am." After taking a reassuring breath, she said, "Jane, I don't know how to ask you this, but I need to borrow your horse and buggy, if I may. I need to get my daughter to urgent care as soon as possible. Penny is mighty sick."

Immediately, Jane's curious expression turned to concern. "What's wrong?"

"She's got a bad fever. It's climbing, too. I'm afraid something's really wrong." Not wanting to waste any more time explaining, she added, "She's home in the house by herself right now. I need to get back to her as soon as I can."

"Of course you need to do that. And of course you can borrow my horse and buggy." Looking at Levi, she said, "Are you going to drive them?"

He nodded. "*Jah*. Thank you for your help. If I wasn't afraid it would take too long, I'd go to my family's barn and get one of our horses and buggies."

"I understand. No worries, anyhow. I wasn't about to go out in this weather." Her voice firm, Jane looked at Levi. "I'll go out to the barn with ya to help you hitch up Sam. He's a *gut* horse, but a little shy around strangers."

"*Danke*." Turning to Julia, he said, "Go on home and get Penny ready. And put something on your head, too. I'll be there as soon as I can."

She was so grateful, she didn't even mind him sounding so heavy-handed. "*Danke,* Levi." Quickly, she turned to Jane. "Thank you, again. I appreciate this so much. I'll do my best to look after Sam, too."

"No need to thank me. That's what neighbors are for, after all."

After giving one more grateful smile, Julia hurried back down the sidewalk. The moment she got inside her house, she hurried to her daughter's room, worried that she'd somehow gotten worse in the time she'd been alone.

But instead, Penny was lying listlessly right where Julia had left her. She opened her eyes when Julia approached the bed.

Julia ran a hand across her brow. She was still burning up. "Penny, let's get you up and dressed, dear," she said softly. "We're going to go see the *doktah*."

Penny shifted to a sitting position. "Did you find a buggy, Mommy?"

"I did. And guess what? Levi is going to take us."

When Penny only nodded, Julia's worries grew by leaps and bounds. In their brief conversations, Penny loved seeing Levi. For her to react so listlessly, she had to be even sicker than Julia thought.

She forced herself to stop worrying and simply focus on what had to be done. She pulled out her daughter's favorite light-blue flannel dress, slipped it carefully on and buttoned it closed. Then she brushed back her hair, fashioning it into a neat bun, and slipped on her *kapp*. Next came thick black tights and her boots.

Penny helped her, but it was as if her limbs were made of stuffed cotton. Julia was reminded of dressing a doll.

When she saw the buggy in the drive, Julia grabbed her purse, placed her black bonnet on her head, then lifted Penny into her arms and carried her outside. The cold beat against their cheeks, causing Penny to tremble.

Levi was right there, taking her child from her and lifting Penny into his arms. Without a word, he set her on the bench seat, then held out a hand to help Julia get inside, too.

Jane had thoughtfully left a pair of thick wool afghans to curl up in. While Levi walked over to his side, Julia wrapped one of them securely around her daughter.

When Levi got in, he looked at her in concern. "You good?"

"*Jah.*"

"All right, then." He unlocked the brake and guided Sam into a slow circle so they could go back down the drive.

None of them said a word as Levi carefully guided the buggy down the snowy street. The metal wheels on the buggy skidded a bit, but

Levi's careful handling of the horse kept her feeling safe.

Vaguely, she noticed that Sam didn't seem bothered by the snow or the cold. He had on a horse blanket, and he actually looked rather happy to be out and about in the weather.

Levi was focused completely on the horse, the road, and the few vehicles they passed. Julia was starting to think that nothing fazed him. She doubted that there was anything he couldn't take care of with ease.

He was certainly a man in a million, at least in her eyes.

She hoped that whomever he courted one day would be worthy of him.

She would have considered herself blessed to have a man like that, indeed.

Chapter 18

❄ ❄ ❄

After mindlessly flipping through magazines for over half an hour, Levi breathed a sigh of relief when he spied Julia and Penny standing at a counter by the waiting room.

"It's good you brought her in, Mrs. Kemp," the doctor said. "I know you are worried, but the antibiotics should help Penny feel better in no time. The pain reliever will allow her to rest, too."

Glad that the English doctor was taking the time to reassure Julia, Levi got to his feet. Julia's face had been pale when he drove her to the clinic in the buggy—and so scared and worried, she was on the verge of tears when they entered the waiting room.

Luckily, the office staff had immediately done everything they could to ease her mind. The receptionist answered her nervous questions and had even allowed Levi to fill out most of the paperwork. They also seemed to rush to get Penny into an examining room.

After a nurse had escorted them down the hall, he'd spoken to Sandy, the receptionist. "Send me the bill, okay, Sandy?" he asked quietly. "Julia's got enough to worry about today."

"Of course, Mr. Kinsinger. Do you want me to send the bill to your office or house?"

"Send it to the mill, care of me. I'll write you a check right away."

"Of course, Mr. Kinsinger."

Satisfied that was taken care of, he took a seat in the waiting room and occupied himself by watching the clock.

As the minutes slowly ticked by, Levi found himself praying that the doctors and nurses would not only see his little neighbor quickly but would see that Penny's mother needed some extra patience and care, too.

He'd also allowed himself to wonder more about Julia's past. She'd seemed so distraught about a fever that he'd been a little surprised by her reaction. Had her husband been so nurturing that his widow had a difficult time handling the needs of her sick daughter?

If so, that would explain how reticent she seemed to be with him. Maybe she simply wasn't used to handling much on her own.

Vaguely remembering how his own father had fussed over his mother, especially when she was ill, Levi hoped that was the case. His parents had had a good marriage and had taken care of each other in a multitude of ways. He hoped Julia and her husband had leaned on each other as much.

When he saw Julia and Penny step closer, Levi was brought back to the present. He immediately stood up, anxious to hear what the doctor's prognosis was.

"*Danke*, Doctor," Julia said as she stopped in front of the receptionist's desk. "I am grateful for your help and time."

The doctor, who didn't look that much older than he or Julia, smiled comfortingly. "No need to thank me for that. That's what we're here for." Pointing to the stack of business cards on the reception desk, he said, "I know you don't have a phone at home, but go ahead and take one of our business cards anyway. We always have a doctor on call. If Penny's fever doesn't go down by tomorrow afternoon, give us a call."

"*Danke*. I will do that."

"Feel better, Penny," he said as he handed her a small purple stuffed dog. "Christmas is coming. You don't want to be sick on Christmas morning, do you?"

"*Nee*," Penny replied.

Just as the doctor turned around, he spied Levi. "Hey, it's good to see you, Levi. Are you feeling under the weather, too?"

"No, sir," Levi replied as he walked closer. "I'm here with Julia and Penny. I drove them here."

"I'm glad they didn't travel here alone in the snow." His eyes twinkled. "I heard through the grapevine that you were in Florida. Are you back for good or just for the holidays?"

"I'm back for good."

"Bet it is going to take some time to adjust to these chilly temperatures!" He grinned at his quip before asking, "How is your family?"

"We're *gut*, Dr. Fergusen. Right now, no one is sick or injured."

"Amelia's leg is feeling good as new?"

"So good she's engaged to be married."

Dr. Fergusen laughed. "Give her my best. No, give your whole family my best. Merry Christmas."

"*Jah.* Merry Christmas," Levi said as he held out Penny's cloak. "Let's get you warm for our ride home."

As he helped her put on her black bonnet, cloak and scarf, Julia looked at him gratefully. "I'm so glad you came outside when I was walking to Jane's *haus*."

"Me, too." Actually, he was feeling so possessive over the two of them, he knew he would have hated to discover that she'd relied on someone else to get them to the clinic and back. "Now let's get Penny back to her own bed."

Looking over at Penny, who had gone into the waiting room while the doctor had been talking to Levi, and was now sitting quietly and playing with her new stuffed dog, Julia smiled. "She already looks better. I'm so relieved."

"I am, too."

"Oh! Goodness, I almost forgot to pay my bill. I'll be right there, Levi."

"Wait, Julia," he said. "Actually—"

"Actually, it's taken care of," the receptionist blurted, with a smile in Levi's direction.

Julia looked completely confused. Stepping closer to the desk, she said, "How can that be?"

"Well . . ." Levi began just as Sandy, the receptionist, piped up again.

"Mr. Kinsinger took care of it."

"You are paying my bill?" Julia turned her head to stare at him. "Why would you do that?"

He was starting to realize she wasn't all that pleased about what he'd done. Hoping to alleviate her worries, he shrugged. "It was nothing."

"*Nee*, it was something. Actually, I'm not sure that—"

"We'll talk about it later," he said. "Not here."

Either she was responding to his firm tone or because she also wasn't eager to discuss his payment of her bill in the middle of the reception area, she nodded.

But just as they were about to get on their way, the receptionist called out her name.

"I'm sorry, Mrs. Kemp. I almost forgot to ask you about the form."

She turned and walked back to the desk. "What is wrong?"

"Well, I was entering your information in the computer, but I'm a little confused." Holding out the paper, she said, "It says Penny's last name is Kemp, but it looks like you told the nurse it was Brubacher."

Julia froze. "Say again?"

"There's some confusion with Penny's last name," Sandy said patiently.

Since Julia still looked stunned, Levi tried to push off the concern. "I'm sure the nurse made a mistake," he said easily.

Sandy shook her head. "No, Kimber wouldn't have done that."

"Julia, what's Penny's last name?" he joked before realizing that something strange was going on. Julia was still looking like she'd been hit by a truck. She was standing motionless and her face was stark white.

"You okay?" he whispered, and gestured for Penny to go sit down again as he rested a hand on her back and leaned closer. "What's wrong? Are you feeling ill, too?"

Sandy, however, seemed to be oblivious to Julia's sudden paleness. She was still looking at the papers in front of her. "Did your husband adopt your daughter? Is that the reason for the different last names?"

"*Nee*," she whispered.

The woman's head popped up. Looking at Julia carefully, she lowered her voice and looked a little embarrassed. "I'm sorry, Mrs. Kemp. I don't want to make you uncomfortable, I'm just trying to make sure I have the correct information. All of our records are in a broad database now, you know. Even with Mr. Kinsinger paying your bill, we still have to have the correct information. What is your daughter's legal last name?"

"Brubacher," Julia whispered. "Penny's name is Penny Brubacher."

Sandy immediately made the notation on the form. "So hers is Brubacher and yours is Kemp," she said loudly, as if she was pleased that her mystery had been solved.

"*Nee.*" Sounding as if she was out of breath, Julia said, "Brubacher is my legal last name, too. Penny has never had a father."

Levi gaped at her. Before he could stop himself, he said, "What?"

Looking more frustrated, Julia sighed. "I mean, of course Penny has a father, but he isn't in the picture. I . . . ah, I've never been married."

"I see." The receptionist looked stricken. "I am sorry, Mrs. Kemp. I mean, Miss Brubacher." Her cheeks turned pink. "Goodness. I'm sorry to bring all this up like that. I . . . well, I was simply trying to make sure I was entering in the correct information."

"I understand," Julia said quietly. "Do you need to know anything else right now?"

Sandy shook her head. "No. We're all set here."

Julia took a deep breath. "*Gut.*"

It was most likely his imagination, but suddenly Levi felt like he was staring at a complete stranger. The woman standing in front of him seemed older. Shy and withdrawn. Almost like the shell of herself.

"May we go now, Levi?" she asked, her voice tight and cold.

"Of course." He walked over to Penny, saw that she was almost asleep, and scooped her up into his arms.

It didn't seem like Julia noticed that her little girl was finally resting or that she now accepted Levi enough to trust him to carry her.

Instead, she opened the door and waited for him to pass through. Then she remained silent while they walked down the hall, out into the snow.

Without a word, she helped him brush off the snow from the buggy and get the horse backed out from the buggy stall and settled.

Only when he was driving the buggy back to Jupiter Street, and Penny was sound asleep, sprawled across her lap, did she speak.

"I am sure you are confused about my name and my past. But I'd rather not discuss it. Just tell me how much I need to reimburse you for the doctor's visit. I'll give you the cash right away."

Levi couldn't believe it. She was acting as if what had just come out in the open wasn't any of his business. "And that's it?"

"*Jah.*" Still looking straight ahead, she nodded. "I think that is for the best."

He was so hurt by the way she was shutting him

out, he blurted, "What is for the best? You keeping your secrets?"

"If that's how you want to describe it, *jah*."

"Does Penny know that you've lied about her name?"

"*Nee.*"

Still unable to abide by her wishes, he let another question fly. "When were you going to tell her? Don't you think she has a right to know who she is?"

"Of course. But she's only five. I hope you will keep my secret."

"It ain't a secret anymore. The receptionist knows. Someone could have overheard, or she could tell someone."

"Hopefully, she won't. If she does tell someone, I will handle it then."

"How?" he asked as he carefully pulled the reins so they could stop at a light.

"Levi, as much as I appreciate your concern, I need to remind you that this isn't your business."

He hadn't thought a woman as sweet as she could dismiss him so easily. "I thought it was," he replied, taking care to not sound as hurt as he felt. "I thought there was something special between us. Was I wrong?"

"Of course not. But this is different."

"How? Julia, you have to have been aware of how I feel about you. You've seen how I live my life. I go to work, see my family, and you. That's it. We are more than friends."

"That is true. And I've valued your friendship. I have." She took a deep breath. "However, that doesn't mean that you can tell me what to do."

"I'm not telling you what to do. I'm simply doing my best to get you to understand that people who have a relationship like ours practice some give and take."

Before she could interrupt him with another weak protest, he added, "Look. I enjoy your company. I think little Penny is adorable. I like that she has begun to smile when she sees me. I like that you smile when you see me! Deny it all you want, but we've become close. All three of us."

"I won't deny that."

Finally, they were getting somewhere. "*Gut.* Then explain to me how we can be so close . . . yet you've felt compelled to lie to me the whole time."

She visibly winced. "Levi, I had to."

She had to? As much as he felt for the pain on her face, he didn't believe that for a second. Everyone had a choice to make. One could either accept what the Lord was asking them to do and deal with it. Or not.

But he'd never thought lying was an option.

Jupiter Street still hadn't been plowed. He slowed Sam's pace to a careful walk. Because of that, it felt like they were moving at a glacial pace. The journey was made even more uncomfortable because Julia looked like she was mad at him.

She was facing front and every muscle in her face looked tense. Perhaps she was.

When he directed Sam up the drive to her house, he said, "Look, why don't you take Penny on inside? I'll take care of the horse and thank Jane."

She warily looked at her front door. "I should probably be the one to tell her thanks."

"You can do that later. Don't you think it's more important for you to take Penny inside?"

"You're right. It is." Shifting, she picked up her purse and glanced his way again. "Are . . . are you going to come over after?"

"*Nee*, I had better get to work. And I think maybe the both of us need to do some thinking."

"Are you terribly mad at me?"

"*Nee*. I'm feeling confused." Needing to settle himself, he leaned his head back against the cold surface of the buggy. "Maybe a little hurt, too, if you want to know the truth."

"I'm sorry. I didn't mean to do that."

He closed his eyes, hearing how empty and distant she sounded. "You know what? I believe you. But as bad as this makes me sound, I have to say that it doesn't make me feel any better."

"I understand." Gathering up her daughter in her arms, she opened the door and stepped out. "*Danke*. Thank you again for your time and trouble today, Levi. It was mighty kind of you to take us. I'll pay you back as soon as I can."

"Don't. I'll be upset if you try and repay me. I'm just glad I was here to help."

Without another word she closed the small buggy door, shifted Penny in her arms, and carried her toward the house.

Levi watched, feeling guilty for feeling betrayed. Perhaps a better man would have simpl assumed that she had a mighty good reason to keep so much from him and moved on.

Unfortunately, he was not that man.

He'd been falling in love with her. Today, he realized that she didn't feel the same way. If she had, she would have been more honest with him. She would have trusted him to keep her secrets safe.

His mind a jumbled mess, he drove the buggy back to the Sheltons' house. He unhitched Sam, then gave him a good brushing before settling him in his stall.

After making sure Sam had fresh hay and water, Levi knocked on Jane's door and thanked her for the use of the horse and buggy.

He walked home and got ready for work. When he started the thirty-minute walk to the mill, he breathed deeply, allowing the crisp, cold air to clean his lungs, and his mind to an extent. He was still torn up about Julia and at a loss about what to do. Should he cajole her into sharing her secrets?

Accept that she didn't trust him completely but continue their relationship?

Realize that the two of them weren't meant to be together?

Unsure of what to do next, he did what he'd always done during a difficult situation. He took comfort in his work. It didn't solve his problems, but work had always made him feel better.

When he walked into the reception area, he smiled at Rebecca. "Sister. Good day."

"You're getting in kind of late today, Levi. Everything okay?"

"*Jah.* I just had a couple of things I needed to handle. They're taken care of now."

She smiled in understanding. "Did you have to do some shopping, too?"

Before he could answer, the door behind him blew open and two men walked in. "We're from Boysen's Mercantile over in Middlefield," one said.

Rebecca fumbled through some papers. "Ah, yes. You had the order for the rocking chairs."

"*Jah*," the burlier one said, looking around the reception area curiously. The man's eyes settled on Levi for a split second before darting away.

His action seemed a bit odd. Levi sized him up. The man looked a little bit rough around the edges. Like some of the men on his team when he'd worked construction down in Pinecraft.

After he watched them converse another

moment or two and seeing nothing amiss, Levi walked down the hall. Moments later, he let himself out the back door of the main building and headed toward his warehouse.

Walking in the cold, he inhaled deeply and realized he wasn't feeling the cold as much as renewed. He was anxious to work.

He didn't know what to think about Julia's lies . . . except that it was painful to realize that she could lie to him so easily.

Instead, he was anxious to think about nothing except work and lumber and the men on his team.

So much so that he almost hoped there was a minor emergency there to handle. Then he would feel like he was in control again. Then, he would feel like he knew what the right thing to do was.

Chapter 19

❄ ❄ ❄

Julia was happy and relieved to be back in the sanctuary of her house, yet her mind kept drifting off as she helped Penny put on a fresh, clean flannel nightgown and get into bed.

More than once Penny had to repeat a question she asked. Julia answered her the best she could, though if she were honest, she was hardly paying attention to her daughter's words.

Penny noticed. "Are you sick too, Mommy?" she finally asked.

"Hmm? *Nee*, child."

"Are you sure? Maybe you've got a fever, too."

"I don't. Now do you need anything else before you take a rest?"

"Just my bear," Penny said in such a way that made Julia realize she'd already asked for it several times.

Walking to her daughter's toy basket, she picked up the well-loved brown bear and handed it to her daughter. "Anything else?"

"*Nee*, Mommy."

Penny sounded so sad, Julia pulled what she hoped was a reassuring smile from somewhere deep inside her. "You'll feel better soon, dear. The *doktah* gave you some *gut* medicine."

"I know."

"Close your eyes, now," she said as she sat down on the edge of the mattress and adjusted her daughter's covers. When Penny exhaled and snuggled deeper into the warm bed, Julia added lightly, "That doctor was mighty nice. The nurses, too. And you were so brave. Why, you hardly flinched when the nurse took a swab of your throat."

Her eyelids peeked open. "Mr. Levi was nice, too."

She couldn't deny that Levi had bent over backward to help then. "Indeed. He was the kindest of all, taking time off work to help us like he did." She ran a hand along Penny's head, smoothing back her hair, which was now splayed out around her in disarray. "When you feel better, we'll make him some cookies as a thank-you."

"What kind?" she asked drowsily. "Peanut butter?"

"Peanut butter cookies sound perfect," she murmured as Penny yawned and rolled to her side.

After waiting another minute or two, Julia got back to her feet and slipped from the room.

With more than a little sense of relief, she closed the door partway, then leaned against the wall. Only then did she allow herself to finally let go.

As if her body had had been waiting for permission, she began to tremble. Fearing she was about to burst into tears, she pressed the back of her head against the wall in a weak attempt to gain support.

How on earth could everything have gone so wrong in one hour's time? Had the Lord intended for her secret to come out like it did . . . or was the blame firmly on her shoulders?

Maybe she'd been careless because she'd been trying to juggle too much. She was working at the notion shop, cleaning Levi's house, helping Penny at school, preparing for Christmas.

Then, of course, there had been Penny's sickness. She'd been so worried about her that she'd let her guard down.

And, unfortunately, everything that she'd been worrying about happening had happened. She'd made a fool of herself at the doctor's office . . . and had disappointed Levi.

Ack, but she was still reeling from the hurt and condemnation she'd seen in his eyes.

At long last, her secret had been uncovered and it had been just as painful and humiliating as she'd imagined it would be.

For as long as she lived, she didn't think she would ever forget the look of dismay and hurt that had appeared on Levi's features. He'd felt betrayed.

In an effort to help herself, she'd been tempted to shake off Levi's feelings of betrayal. It was almost easy to do. Though they'd gotten close, there wasn't a lot between them.

Not really.

They were only neighbors who had been lonely. That loneliness and proximity had fed their relationship.

If she and Penny ran from Charm and started over somewhere else, Levi wouldn't actually miss her, would he? More than once, he'd told her that he was merely biding time until his lease ran out. Then he'd return to his big house and his normal life.

Jupiter Street would be nothing but a memory. No doubt, one day he would forget about the good times they'd had together and the laughter they'd shared.

Maybe he'd forget that they'd been good friends and simply think of her as his maid.

But even as she thought of those things, she knew she wasn't being fair. Yes, they were neighbors who had helped each other. And yes, she had been his maid. But what he'd said in the buggy had been exactly right. They were much more than just neighbors and friends. They'd become a unit. A group of three. She was too afraid to think of them as a type of family. She had to guard her heart too much for that.

But they had certainly become close.

Going into the kitchen, she lit the gas stove, filled a kettle, and got out a mug and tea bag. She was going to allow herself to simply sit and figure out what to do next before she started making Penny some soup.

Sometime today or tomorrow, she was sure that Levi would knock on her door. He was going to demand an explanation. And because she knew he deserved it, she was going to have to do her best to give him one.

When the kettle started to steam, she quickly moved it from the burner to prevent it from whistling and made her tea. Then she wrapped her hands around the mug and sat back down at her small kitchen table and tried to figure out what, exactly, she was going to tell Levi.

Though she was going to tell him the truth, she figured there were various degrees of that truth to tell him. Did she tell him about Luther? Everything about him?

And what about her parents? Should she tell him that she'd left them without anything more than a note because she didn't want to have to see how disappointed they were in her?

Levi was a man who'd already lost both of his parents. She knew he still grieved for them. Would he ever understand that she'd ignored her parents because she was so weak she didn't want to see them look at her in a bad way? Now that so much time had passed, she hardly understood it.

On the other hand, how could she not be completely open and honest with him? To continue to keep things from him seemed like a terrible thing to do. Hurtful, even.

And what would happen if she did tell him

everything and he didn't understand? What if her actions sickened him and he didn't want to know either her or Penny anymore?

Could she face that?

She didn't think so.

And that, unfortunately, made her feel like she was as much at a loss as ever.

Few jobs had ever felt so endless. Luther forced himself to stand off to one side while Bill concluded their business at Kinsinger's mill.

"Thank you for helping us load the chairs," Bill said to Roman, their main contact at the mill. "Without your help, it would have taken Luther and I twice the time to load and secure twelve rocking chairs."

"It weren't no problem. It does my body good to lug these chairs around every now and then," Roman replied with an easy grin. "It's the least I can do. We sure appreciate your business. Let us know if you need to place another order soon. If so, I'll get a team to work on them right away."

"We'll do that," Bill replied. Just as if neither of them had anything else to do. "I'm glad this partnership is working out so well. Our customers can't seem to get enough of your handcrafted chairs and tables."

"It's giving all of us a merry Christmas, for sure," Luther said.

Roman raised a hand. "If we don't see you until the new year, I hope you have a blessed one."

"You, too," Bill said. "Thank you again for the help."

Realizing that they were about to leave and he'd be no closer to discovering whether the woman he'd seen was actually Julia, Luther stepped forward. "Roman, before we leave, I was wondering if you might know a Julia Brubacher? She's blond. And has a child. A girl who is maybe five or six."

"Why do you want to know?"

Roman sounded so suspicious, Luther took care to keep his voice nonchalant. "It's hard to believe, but I think I saw her walking down the street when we were driving. I'm not a hundred percent sure, of course, but she sure looked like a woman I used to know."

"Why didn't you say anything to me when you saw her?" Bill asked. "We could have stopped."

"I didn't want to approach her in our truck if she wasn't Julia," Luther said with a shrug. "She might have gotten spooked or something."

Though Bill smiled like he understood, Roman stared at him curiously. "Any special reason you're asking about this woman? Or why you need to seek her out now?"

Though Roman didn't sound all that happy, he wasn't disregarding Luther's interest, either. He decided to take that as a positive sign. "Julia and

I were once close. She and I went to school together, you see. Then we lost touch."

"And you just happened to see her on the sidewalk in Charm?" Roman's voice had an edge to it now.

"We were once really *gut* friends," he said meaningfully. "Then, well, we got in a small disagreement and started seeing other people. We, ah, lost touch when I got married."

"You are married and asking about her?"

"He's a widower," Bill blurted in an obvious attempt at diffusing the situation.

"Oh. I'm real sorry about your loss," Roman said. For the first time he was looking at Luther with something akin to compassion in his eyes.

"It was a year ago," Luther said. "It's been a hard year, you know? My wife, she died in childbirth." He felt vaguely bad about using his own personal loss as a way to get information, but only slightly. He needed to find his daughter.

Roman looked even more taken aback. "You lost both a child and a wife? Now, that is a shame. I really am sorry."

"*Danke*, but I am surviving." Though his head was telling him to be patient and wait a little longer to discover Julia's whereabouts, there was something deeper inside him that didn't want to let this chance go. "Ah, going back to Julia . . . if you don't know her, no worries. It's just one of those things, you know? We all grow up and move. Lose track of each other." He cleared his throat. "However, I couldn't help but ask since, well, she and I were once friends and now I have no one."

Roman's expression eased. "*Jah.* I do know how that goes. To answer your question, I recently have met a Julia who is new to Charm, but she has a different last name. My wife has taken her under her wing at church. She's blond and has a little girl. Don't know if that's the same woman, but it sure sounds like it might be."

It took everything he had not to raise his hand in triumph. "She might very well be. So, is she married?"

"I don't think so. I'm pretty sure my wife said she was a widow." Brightening, he said, "If she married, that is probably why she has a different name."

"Maybe the Lord knew we needed to find each other," Luther said piously.

Bill slapped him on the back. "Maybe so. Isn't this something?"

Though Roman didn't look as if he completely agreed, he nodded slowly.

"Do you know where she lives?" Luther pressed. "I'd like to pay her a visit."

Fresh apprehension—as well as no small amount of indignation—entered Roman's eyes. "I do not know where she lives. But surely you wouldn't think I'm the kind of man who would give out women's addresses to strangers?"

Feeling frustrated, Luther gritted his teeth. "Of course not," he bit out at last. "But then, I didn't think I was a stranger."

Roman crossed his arms over his chest. "You ain't, but we are far from friends."

Luther could feel his temper taking hold of him. "What are we, then? How well do you have to know a person before you bend a little bit and help him?"

Now Bill was staring at him as if he was peculiar. "Let's go, Luther," he said quickly. "We've got to grab something to eat and head back before nightfall."

"But—"

Bill gripped his shoulder. "We gotta go. Now."

Luther freed his shoulder with a jerk but took care to temper his expression. "Yeah. All right. Thanks for your help."

"It was no problem," Roman said. But he stared at Luther a little too closely and didn't move until they walked through the door.

Feeling the man's gaze settling on him intently, Luther knew then that he'd made an error in judgment. He'd been too pushy. So intent on getting his information that Roman was going to remember his asking.

He might even tell Julia that a man like him was asking about her. Then she might run.

Thinking about how angry he was going to be at

her when he finally got her to himself, Luther thought she was going to regret ever sneaking off in the first place.

As they got in the truck, Bill glared at him. "What was that all about?"

"Nothing. It was exactly like you heard."

"I don't think so. It sounded like something else."

"Like what?"

Seeing the anger in his eyes, Bill backed down. "I don't know, but it was odd. You should watch yourself, man. The boss is making a lot of money off these chairs, and in this economy, that's a good thing. If you do something to tick off our supplier, he ain't going to be happy."

"I didn't tick off anyone."

"I hope not," Bill said. "I really hope you didn't."

"Let's just eat and get on back," Luther said as he stared out the window.

Bill turned on the engine and pulled out of the parking lot. Irritation was practically emanating from him.

However, Luther didn't care. If Bill wasn't talking, then Luther could concentrate on staring at each person they passed. Sooner or later, he was going to see Julia again.

And when he did, she was going to be very sorry.

Chapter 20

❄❄❄

December 17

The knock came bright and early the next day.

After peeking to make sure her visitor was Levi, Julia opened the door. "I didn't expect to see you again so soon."

"I couldn't help myself. But after work last night, I kept looking over here from my front window, thinking about Penny and—"

"And what you discovered about my past?"

"*Jah.* I couldn't help but spend quite a bit of time thinking about that." He looked around warily. "I know it's only eight in the morning, but can I come in?"

"Of course." She stood back to allow him entrance. As she closed the door, she looked longingly outside. The snow had dissipated overnight and the dawn had brought forth a bright and sunny day. The bright-blue skies shining against the backdrop of snow-covered lawns made even Jupiter Street seem like a beautiful place.

If Penny had been feeling better, she would have been anxious to go outside and build a snowman.

While Levi looked around the room awkwardly, she hastily picked up the quilt that she was stitching. Because it was so big, she'd had it—and her eyeglasses, needle, thimbles, and thread—strewn all over the couch and coffee table. "Sorry. I've been trying to get this quilt stitched before Christmas."

He ran a hand over the white-on-white quilt. "It's pretty. Is it a gift?"

"*Nee.* I'm hoping to sell it before Christmas."

"For extra money?"

"Well, yes. Like I told you, I have been hoping to buy Penny the doll she wants."

For some reason, that seemed to make Levi even more uncomfortable. "Would you like something to drink?" she offered. "Tea? Coffee?"

"Nothing, thank you."

"Then perhaps we should just sit down."

After he did as she asked, he rested both of his palms on his thighs and stared at her solemnly. "I've got a lot of questions, but only one that I really hope you'll answer."

Feeling sick to her stomach, she nodded. "I'm ready."

"How is Penny feeling?"

Startled, but feeling so relieved, she blinked back tears. This was why she'd risked so much to be close to Levi Kinsinger.

He'd gone out of his way to help her, discovered she'd been lying to him about many things, and wasn't happy about it, either. But instead of getting mad at her, he focused on what was most important—her daughter's health.

"She . . . she's doing better, I think. She only woke up once last night and went back to sleep fairly soon after I gave her some more pain reliever."

"And her fever?"

"It's now lingering at one hundred degrees. Not fantastic, of course, but not scary like it was before."

He exhaled. "I'm glad about that."

"I am, too." Feeling better than she had for the last twelve hours, she smiled wanly. "Is there anything else you want to talk about?" Maybe he was feeling the same as she and didn't want to revisit what had happened in the doctor's office.

"There is. Julia, I'd very much like to know why."

And just like that, trepidation engulfed her again. "Why what?" she asked nervously.

"Why everything. I'm not naïve about the world, Julia. If you felt like you had a good reason for keeping your identity a secret, I'm sure you did. But I'd like to hear it."

She knew she had to tread carefully. But she also knew she owed it to him to tell the truth. Though there wasn't much of a decision to be made, she briefly thought about not sharing all of her past with him.

She knew she was doing this out of purely selfish reasons. She hated the thought of him looking at her in disgust. Or even pity. She wanted him to still see her as a capable woman.

Thinking back to her locked door and her need for a buggy, she mentally amended her descriptor. A capable woman who needed a little help.

She was going to have to tell him everything. No way did she want to give him her past history in increments. All that would happen would be to make him distrust her.

And they would no doubt be having the same conversation again.

But she still had to prepare him. "What I have to tell you . . . it ain't pretty."

"I don't need pretty. Just the truth."

"All right." She exhaled as she tried to figure out where to begin. She looked down at her clenched hands. "Well, you see . . . back when I was a teenager, I was an outgoing girl. I had my share of friends, some of which were boys."

"Where was this?"

"In Middlefield. I have an older sister and two kind, supportive parents. They were always good to me."

"Were?" When she lifted her chin to meet his gaze, he asked, "Are they deceased?"

"Oh, no. They are still living."

A line formed between his brows. "But they weren't here for Thanksgiving."

"I, ah . . . well, I don't talk to them."

"You don't talk to them."

"*Nee.* They don't know about my name change. They don't even know where I'm living."

He leaned back on the couch. "I see."

Though he didn't sound especially judgmental, he didn't sound all that understanding, either. And that made her feel even more nervous. "As I was saying, I had some admirers and had been rather sheltered. When I met Luther, who was older and much sought after, I was a bit starstruck."

She rushed on before Levi could question her motivations. She wasn't proud of them and didn't think they could stand up to his questioning. "I, well, I fear I let my pride and vanity get the best of me. When Luther acted as if everything I did was pleasing and good, I thought it was because he thought I was better than the other women in our circle of friends."

She hated how that made her sound. So flighty and full of herself. She was so embarrassed, she looked back down at her hands. She didn't dare meet Levi's eyes now.

After a couple of seconds, he said, "What happened next?"

"Luther started courting me in earnest. He was attentive and sweet. Almost too much. He started wanting me with him all the time, as much as my parents would allow."

"And did they allow it?"

"*Jah.* My sister had been courted and was married so they thought they knew what to expect. When he asked my parents for my hand in marriage, they gave it freely. After all, that was what I wanted, too, and they trusted me. You see, I had always been a good and obedient girl. They had no reason to suspect I would do anything to disappoint them." She bit her lip. Now every action she remembered could be seen in a different, far less flattering light.

"Did you disappoint them?"

"Oh, yes." Gathering her courage, she turned her head to face Levi. "When Luther wanted to . . . well, have sex before marriage . . . the night we got engaged, I allowed it."

A wrinkle formed in his forehead. "Did he force you, Julia? Bully you?"

She knew what he was after. He was looking for a way to excuse her from any responsibility. But she wasn't going to do that. Everything that happened to her was her fault and no one else's. "*Nee.*"

Something in his expression cleared, then became more contemplative. "Ah. If you were not hurt, what happened? Why did you run? Did he not want to marry you?"

"He still wanted me. I'm the one who changed her mind."

Levi's expression was so shocked, she could

tell he was having a difficult time keeping his opinions to himself. "I expect you had a reason," he said.

However, his voice was full of doubt.

She didn't blame his skepticism. She needed to tell him the whole story, even if it hurt to share.

Steeling her spine, she said, "Soon after we did what we did, things changed. Luther tried getting even more possessive. And sometimes cruel. I started trying to guess what would make him happy so he wouldn't get upset with me. But nothing I did was ever good enough. Nothing I ever did seemed to be right."

"So then you ran?"

"Oh, no. I was sure I would win him over, that I would change him."

"But you didn't."

"*Nee.*" Whispering to herself, she said, "I really didn't change him at all. And he became so much more cruel." Forcing herself to continue, she met Levi's gaze. "After we'd been engaged for about six weeks or so, I realized that I was pregnant. One night, when I was figuring out how I was going to tell him the news, he got mad about something I'd done. And he hit me."

He inhaled sharply. "Luther hit you, knowing you were carrying his child?"

"Oh, he never knew, Levi." Folding her arms over her stomach, she said, "It wasn't the first time he'd hit me, but it was the first time he'd left a mark on my face. I had to lie to my parents."

Levi made a noise in the back of his throat.

She didn't dare look at him. Keeping her face averted, she continued. "I knew then that I had to do something. I knew if I told Luther that I was with child, he would be mad. But then he'd make sure I never left his side. So I didn't tell anyone."

"No one? Not even your parents?"

"Especially not them. I couldn't bear to see their disappointed expressions, and I was sure they were going to be disappointed in me."

Levi's voice turned reassuring. "I imagine they would have been, but surely that didn't mean that they wouldn't still love you and want to help."

Needing him to understand, Julia looked at him again. "Levi, you are right but you are also wrong. Yes, they would have still loved me. But they would have encouraged me to overlook Luther's anger."

"Perhaps not."

"I'm not saying they would have forced me to marry him. But they would have strongly encouraged it."

"And if you still said no?"

"Then they would have taken my burdens on their shoulders. I knew my mother well. She would have acted as if my pregnancy was her fault."

His eyebrows lifted. "Surely not."

"She would have blamed herself for not cautioning me more about giving myself before marriage. And because I couldn't let her do that, and because I was so embarrassed, I left."

"I'm trying to understand, but the picture you are painting is rather unusual, don't you think? Maybe they would have treated you that way at first, but time moves forward. People change."

"They do. But all of that would have been a moot point, anyway. Luther would have never allowed me to do anything but marry him. There was no way on earth he would have accepted my refusal of marriage."

"So that is when you ran."

Glad that her story was almost over, she nodded. "I did. I ran one night."

"What did you do? Where did you go? It wasn't around here, was it?"

"*Nee.* I took a bus to Millersburg, found an inexpensive motel that had vacancies and was looking for help, and met two of the kindest people I've ever had the good fortune to know. Connie and Jared hired me on the spot, and even allowed me to sleep in the smallest room in the back of the place that was rarely filled."

Remembering her first nights there, how rested she'd felt because she was no longer in hiding, no longer worrying about what to do, she smiled.

"I felt as if the Lord was with me, Levi. I told them I was Julia Kemp and that I'd recently lost my husband of two years and that I was expecting our first baby."

"They accepted all of your lies."

"They did. But they also accepted me," she said, hoping that maybe, just maybe, Levi would understand what that had meant to her. "I had a good life there at the motel. I worked through my pregnancy and Connie helped me with Penny after she was born. I think they liked having us there. Penny loved them."

"So why did you leave?"

"Because Penny had to start school and Jared and Connie were wanting to retire. It was time to start standing on my own two feet. So I moved here and started over."

She had done it. She had shared her story. Her true story. She felt both sick to her stomach and overwhelmed with relief as she stared at Levi. She had no idea what he was going to say, but she did know that she felt as if a huge burden had been lifted from her shoulders.

Levi leaned back. His handsome face, usually looking vaguely like he was on the verge of laughter, was now looking troubled.

And seeing that, some of the relief she'd been feeling dissipated. He might have known her story now, she might have told him the truth, but that didn't mean he was okay with it all.

"Do you want to know anything else?" she asked. Her voice had a touch of desperation to it. She was realizing that she'd hoped that he'd understand what she did, and why—hoped that he'd forgive her, and that everything between them was going to be okay again.

"*Nee.*" Standing up, he shook his head. "*Danke*, Julia, for sharing your story with me. I should probably be heading home now."

"That's it?" she blurted.

He paused as he slipped on his coat. "What do you want me to say?"

Feeling a bit at a loss, she realized that she wanted him to say a great many things.

She wanted him to say that he understood. That he forgave her for lying to him. She yearned to hear that he thought they could overcome this problem and continue their friendship.

But of course she couldn't put words into his mouth or ask him to feel something he didn't. "I thought you might have had some questions," she said at last.

"I don't know if I do or not." His expression pursed, then relaxed as he spoke again. "I like you, Julia. Actually, I thought I was falling in love with you. With Penny, too. I think you are pretty and sweet. I've liked that I've felt like the two of you needed me. But I am not sure how I feel about you keeping all of this from me."

"I had my reasons."

"I agree. You did. This man sounds terrible."

"He was."

"I would never want you to be hurt. Of course I wouldn't. But I am not sure how I feel about you abandoning your sister and your parents. And, well, shouldn't this man have been told he had a child?"

Panic set in. "If he had found out, he would have taken her!"

"But . . . couldn't you have gone to the police or something? They could have kept him from hurting you. And then . . . people can change. Maybe he would have changed."

"He wouldn't have changed, Levi. I hear what you're saying, but you don't understand what he was like."

"You are right. I don't," he said with regret. "All I know is that I was missing my father so much that I had a difficult time sleeping in my own house. I had to escape to Florida so my siblings wouldn't see how distraught I was. Since I came back, I had to get the house across from you because I still was hurting so much. But you, you walked away from everything five years ago and never looked back."

"Of course I did. It's been hard, Levi."

"I'm sure it has been. But I can't help but wonder if you would have ever told me about your past if it hadn't come out at the doctor's office. Would you have told me?"

She wanted to tell him that she would have. But she wasn't going to lie to him again. "I don't know."

Gazing at her sadly, he said, "That was what I was afraid you'd say." She stood in shock as he quietly walked to the door and opened it. Then walked out without a backward glance.

Feeling more alone than she had in years, Julia took care to lock the door. She was mentally and physically exhausted.

Life sometimes felt so hard.

Chapter 21

❄ ❄ ❄

Later that afternoon

"I appreciate you coming over and helping us put in these bookshelves," Simon said to Levi. "I sure didn't want to tackle these on my own today."

Sitting on the floor of the main room of The Refuge, Levi shook off his buddy's thanks. "You know this is no trouble, especially since your sister elected to use a kit instead of depending on fine Amish craftsmanship."

Tess, who was unloading books, glared at him. "Just because these aren't beautiful, it doesn't mean that they won't do the job just fine. They were cheap."

"We wouldn't have charged you full price, Tess."

"I'm sure these were still less expensive than Amish-made."

Holding up two of the flimsy boards, Levi couldn't resist teasing her a little more. "They're certainly less everything. I'm not even sure what they're made of."

"They'll do the job, for sure. They just won't

look too good," Simon interjected. "Honestly, Tess, you need to start asking me for things."

"I did. I asked you to install the shelves."

Levi chuckled as he picked up another bracket and tried to match it to the diagram drawn on the inside of the box. "I'm thinking we should stop needling Tess. Pick up a screwdriver, Simon. We've got things to do."

Grumbling under his breath, Simon did as Levi asked and concentrated on working by Levi's side.

Together, they measured, screwed in bolts, put shelves in place, then did it again. It was painstaking work and not a little bit frustrating, since many of the angles didn't match up perfectly.

However, it was also easy enough, and the perfect remedy for his wandering mind. Simon's request for help had been a welcome reprieve from what he'd been doing ever since he'd walked home from Julia's house. He hadn't been able to do much besides try not to gaze out the window at Julia's front door.

He was so confused. When he'd met Julia, he'd thought she was a breath of fresh air. She'd seemed sweet and honest, a woman who, like him, had overcome some personal tragedies not of her making.

He had been sure that she was someone he could trust and eventually form a close relationship with. Oh, who was he kidding? He'd become smitten from practically the first moment he'd laid eyes on her. Sure, she was pretty, but she was so much more than that. She was sweet and kind. She was also a survivor. She had faced more than her share of difficult moments yet had somehow retained an innocence and an air of hopefulness about her.

She'd made him want to cast aside his grief and hurt and count his blessings.

And then there was Penny. That little girl was adorable and carried many of the same traits that he'd admired in her mother. She made him want to give her a home and a family like the one he'd been raised in. She also inspired him to be the type of man Julia needed by her side to raise her daughter.

He'd known that Julia was the person he'd been waiting for. He knew that with her affection and love, he'd finally be able to move forward. Her story had reminded him that he wasn't the only person in the world to have experienced grief at an early age. All in all, Julia's story had made him want to be stronger, to work harder, to love more easily.

He'd made her up to be his beacon. Maybe he'd even made her be perfect in his mind.

But she wasn't. She was just as imperfect and human as he was.

All of those things were why it was so hard to wrap his mind around much of what she'd told him had been made-up stories.

While he'd been trusting her enough to reveal his many weaknesses, she hadn't felt the same way.

Instead of being his salvation, Julia had become yet another obstacle in his life. And though it wasn't fair of him, he was angry about it, too.

In his weakest moments, he was tempted to lash out and tell the world that she was nothing like what she seemed.

But how could he knowingly ruin her life, or more importantly, ruin little Penny's life? She was a victim.

But if he said nothing to anyone about her past, was that making him as bad as she was?

And what about Penny's father? Surely, he had a right to know about his own flesh and blood. Just as quickly, darker thoughts intervened. What if Julia had been telling the truth and this man, this Luther, really was as mean and abusive as she'd said? Levi needed to protect them, not hurt them further.

No matter which way Levi looked at the situation, there seemed to be both pros and cons. He was confused and at a loss of what to do next. Yet again, he wished his father was still alive. His father had not only been a good businessman, he'd also had an instinctive way of knowing how to judge people and situations.

Heaving a heavy sigh, Simon shifted positions. *Jah*, his father would have definitely known what to do next. He would have listened to Levi's opinions, too. Then, somehow, some way, his father would have guided Levi to make the right decision, even going so far as to help Levi imagine that he'd thought of the solution all on his own in the first place.

Now Levi didn't know who to discuss this dilemma with. He didn't want to hurt Julia's feelings by talking about her. He also didn't know if he could handle his siblings' opinions if they judged Julia too harshly.

Actually, he was pretty sure he would lose his temper if anyone spoke unkindly to her.

"Hey, Levi?" Simon asked. "You okay?"

He inhaled sharply, then pretended that he'd been lost in thought. "Sure. Why?"

"You've been staring off into space for the last couple of minutes. All the while looking like you've lost your best friend in the world."

Straightening, Levi attempted to look a whole lot more positive than he felt. "I'm fine. I just had a difficult conversation with someone this morning that I can't seem to stop thinking about. Every time I think I've shaken it off, I remember something else about it. Worse, I'm pretty sure I'm about to hurt that person's feelings."

"I hate when that happens," Tess said. "I used to do that with work calls and appointments all the time."

Levi hadn't exactly expected Tess to chime in, but he figured she was as good as anyone to get a sense of what to do next. "Not knowing what to do is wearing me out. How did you stop thinking about it?"

"Since it was work, I usually just concentrated on the issue and took things one step at a time. It was easiest to only concentrate on each task instead of worrying about things I couldn't control." Turning her head so that she was looking him in the eye, she said, "Can you do that?"

"Thank you, but not really. This has nothing to do with work."

"Want to talk about it?" Simon asked.

Wanting to talk about it—and feeling able—were two different things. "*Nee.* I couldn't share the conversation even if I wanted to. It's personal."

Simon's hazel eyes settled on him. "You know I would never betray your trust."

"I know that, Simon. But this news, well, it is kind of disturbing."

"You know, too, that there ain't much that is going to shock me," he said drily. "I'm not an innocent. Not by a long shot."

"This is true." Simon had left Charm at fifteen, fought for money, gotten into drugs, and eventually had even spent time in prison before straightening out his life and returning to Charm.

"You could share the gist of it, at the very least," Simon prodded. "Sometimes talking about what's bothering you helps."

"My brother is right," Tess said sympathetically.

"If you two want to talk here, I can leave the room. I don't mind giving you some privacy."

Levi hadn't intended on ever saying a word about Julia to anyone, but he was thinking they probably did have a point. Talking about what was on his mind would help. And, well, there couldn't be two less judgmental people in Charm. Both Tess and Simon had overcome a great many trials over the years.

"I think you two might have a point. I fear I'm hurting someone I truly care about. I need to fix things or come to terms with the fact it is all out of my control."

"I'll go to the other room so you can have some privacy," Tess said.

As she moved to go, Levi said, "No, stay here, Tess. Since you're a woman, maybe you could help me figure something out."

Simon smiled. "Ah, woman troubles."

"It involves a woman, but it's not what you're thinking."

"I still have had my share of worries about figuring out what is on a woman's mind."

Only half teasing, Levi raised a hand in protest. "If you are going to start sharing things about my little sister, don't."

"I wouldn't dare. Besides, I have no troubles with Amelia." Right then and there, all humor faded from his expression as he stared at Levi intently. "You know that."

Levi blinked. Simon was known to most as a fairly easygoing man. He liked to tease and joke around from time to time, too. However, he never joked about his devotion to Amelia. Ever. He was really and truly head over heels in love with Levi's sister. It made him both extremely happy for her and a bit uncomfortable, too. Amelia was wonderful. He'd always thought so. But what was it about her that inspired Simon to hold her in such high esteem?

Tess walked over and sat cross-legged by Levi's side. Her jeans were faded and she had on thick red socks under her heavy-soled boots. The cheerful socks reminded him of Julia's red-and-green socks, which a friend had made for her.

"So, did you have a problem with Julia?" she prodded.

"Jah." Deciding to start somewhere, he said, "Her daughter, Penny, has strep throat. She developed a terrible fever yesterday and Julia needed some help. I borrowed a neighbor's buggy and took them to the clinic."

"Okay," Simon said. "Then what?"

"Don't be so impatient, Simon," Tess chastised. Softening her voice, she asked, "Is Penny okay?"

"I think so. The doctor gave her some medicine. Julia took her home to rest. But it was while I was at the doctor's office that I learned something." Choosing each word carefully, he said, "It was a secret that I wasn't supposed to find out."

"What was it?"

Hoping he was doing the right thing, he said quietly, "I discovered that Julia is not really a widow at all. She pretended to be a widow to cover up the fact that she had a baby out of wedlock."

Warily, he looked at Tess and Simon, steeling himself to see two twin expressions of shock.

But instead of that, they just looked sad.

"Poor thing," Tess said.

" 'Poor thing'?" he repeated. "She's been lying to me. She told me she was a widow, but she's never been married."

"*Jah*. We got that." Simon's eyes were serious.

Levi looked from one to the other. "You two don't seem to be very surprised. Or, well, shocked."

"I am surprised," Simon said. "I only met Julia once. She seemed like a nice lady. It's too bad that she's had to raise her daughter on her own. I bet it has been hard." Looking at Levi directly, he said, "As far as being shocked, I'm kind of having a hard time understanding why you are so upset. I can only guess that she's saying she's a widow because of her daughter. And her daughter is five or six, right?"

"She is."

"Then, whatever happened to make Julia tell people she was a widow happened years ago. Isn't it a little late for you to be so judgmental?"

"I'm not being judgmental," he said quickly,

just as he realized that he absolutely had been. He'd been acting like the sort of person he despised, casting stones without thought to the damage he was inflicting.

Tess cleared her throat. "I may not still be Amish, but I know how things work in the Amish community. People might not approve, but she wouldn't have been shunned. These things happen."

"There's more," he blurted. "She has a fake name."

While Simon's expression turned blank, Tess's grew more concerned. "Why did she take on a fake name?"

"She revealed that the man she was engaged to hurt her. She didn't want him to ever find Penny."

"She's been on the run this whole time?" Tess reached out and grabbed his arm. "Oh, Levi. You should tell her about this place. She could talk to some people and get help."

Yet again, she was missing the point. "Tess, she's been lying to me about who she is. I fell—" He stopped abruptly, realizing that he was about to tell them that he'd fallen in love with a woman who hadn't cared enough to tell him the truth about who she was.

"It sounds like she had a good reason, Levi," she whispered. "Sometimes people are in such bad situations that the only thing they can do is lie about who they are."

"I hear you." He sighed. "Obviously, she's been frightened and having to make choices that I've never had to make."

"But your feelings are hurt," Simon said.

"Yeah." At last daring to verbalize his secret, he said, "I fell in love with a woman I didn't know nearly as well as I thought. Facing Simon, he sighed. "And that is what has got me so spun up. I feel frustrated with her. I also feel frustrated with myself for fixating on my pain instead of only caring about hers."

Tess got to her feet. "I . . . excuse me, I need to run up to my room for a moment."

As they listened to her run upstairs, Levi said, "I'm sorry, I didn't mean to upset her."

"I don't think you did. I, ah, think she was trying to give you some space." After a pause, he added, "And, she might have been a little bit afraid to say too much."

"So she thinks I'm being upset for no reason."

"I don't know what she thinks," Simon said evenly. "I am only just getting to know her again, remember?"

"All right, then. What do you think?"

"Truthfully?"

"Of course."

"I think that you are looking at the leaves and not the tree from which they came from."

"Oh, for heaven's sakes! English, please."

"Levi, you are focusing on the wrong things.

You keep saying that Julia hid herself from you, but I don't know if that's the case. She might have given you the wrong last name, but it sounds as if she gave you herself, too."

"I am beginning to realize that, too."

"What did she lie about that really matters? Is she a good mother or do you think she's secretly mistreating Penny?"

The idea of Julia hurting her daughter was almost laughable. "She's a *gut mudder*. The best."

"You said she works at the notion store with Angel and has been cleaning your house for extra money. Is that the case?"

"You know it is."

"Is she lying and stealing and presenting a different person to the rest of the world than to you?"

"You know she is not."

"Then if she is the person who you know her to be, but has been hiding her past because she doesn't want people to be judgmental, and she changed her last name because she doesn't want the person who hurt her to hurt her again . . . is that all really so bad?"

As Simon's words sunk in, Levi blinked. His friend had been exactly right. She'd covered up a past that really didn't affect him.

She was essentially the same person he'd always known her to be.

Actually, the only thing that had changed was

the fact that when she'd taken a chance to share her secrets, he'd made every fear she had justified. He'd been judgmental and rigid. He'd hurt her feelings because he'd wanted her to be perfect.

But no one was perfect, most especially not him.

He'd also forced the conversation when he'd known she was tired and exhausted and her daughter was sick. Then he'd left, feeling self-righteous and justified.

"I've been terrible," he whispered. "She told me her story reluctantly but with hope that I would understand. But instead of understanding anything, I concentrated on all the wrong things. What is worse is that I was so hurt—because I knew I had fallen in love with her. But instead of . . ." His voice trailed off.

"I don't know what you want to do next, but I wouldn't be too hard on yourself," Simon said slowly. "You haven't had the experiences that I have. When I was living on the streets and in prison, I met people whose lives had been so horrific that they changed their names in an attempt to do anything to be able to start over in life." He shrugged. "I'm not excusing anything, but I would be lying if I said I didn't understand what would motivate someone to make a fresh start."

Levi appreciated his viewpoint, but that wasn't what was bothering him. "No, I need to be hard on myself because the worst part about what I did, Simon, is that I treated Julia like that even knowing that I'd fallen in love with her. What kind of a man treats the woman he loves like that?"

"Not you," Simon said softly. "Go back to her and apologize. Tell her that you weren't thinking clearly, or something. If she loves you, too, she'll forgive you."

"I hope you're right."

"I know I am." Looking pleased, Simon said, "After all, your sister has forgiven me for my past."

"This is true."

Pointing to the door, Simon said, "Go on out of here. I've got these shelves. You've got something more important to do."

"*Danke.*" He was just putting on his coat when Simon called out his name. "What is it?"

Simon walked toward him, a brightly colored pamphlet in his hand. "If you do go see Julia, you might want to give her this. It's information about The Refuge. Even though she isn't a woman in jeopardy, she might want someone to talk to who has been in the same situation. Tess can give her some information about different groups for battered women."

Taking the pamphlet, he folded it neatly and placed it in his pocket. If she didn't want to talk to him, he could write a note and set it in her mailbox.

It was time to make amends and to make them count.

Chapter 22

❄ ❄ ❄

Sunday, December 18

"*Mommi*, are you sick, too?"

Julia had just taken Penny's temperature and was relieved to see it had lowered to ninety-nine degrees. It was still a little high, but they were now out of the danger zone. She had just been about to praise the Lord when her daughter's little voice caught her off guard.

She looked at Penny curiously. Her daughter was curled up under her quilts, hugging her teddy bear tightly. She was staring at Julia like she was fearful that something terrible was going to happen. "What makes you ask such a thing?"

She pointed to Julia's eyes. "Your eyes are all watery and red. Maybe your strep throat is there."

Julia didn't know whether to laugh or cry some more. Because, of course, that was what her problem had been. She'd been crying off and on for most of the night.

Hoping she sounded better than she felt, she said, "One cannot get strep throat in one's eyes, silly."

"Only in your throat?"

"Only in your throat. And my throat is fine."

"Then how come your eyes are all red and watery?"

It was times like this when Julia was reminded about how isolated she and Penny were. Penny often dwelled on the fact that it was only the two of them in the world. Because of that, she was always a little afraid that something would happen to her mother.

Quickly, Julia sought to reassure her. "I had a hard time sleeping. My eyes are tired because they want to rest. Sometimes they water when they get like that."

"How come you couldn't sleep?" Looking anxious, she said, "Was it because I was sick?"

Brushing a few loose strands away from her daughter's face, she shrugged. "Maybe a little bit. I don't like it when you are feeling poorly."

"I'm better now."

"That you are." She got to her feet. "Now, what sounds good to eat? Do you want some applesauce or cream of wheat?"

"Applesauce with cinnamon."

"I'll go get you some. Maybe later you can have some soup."

"*Mamm*?"

She turned back to Penny. "*Jah*?"

"If you weren't crying because of me being sick, why were you so sad?"

"I'm a grown-up. Sometimes I worry about

grown-up things." She leaned closer and pressed her lips to her daughter's forehead. "And, because you are a little girl, you don't need to worry about those things."

Penny stared at her hard, bit her lip, then blurted, "Were you thinking about my *daed*?"

Julia was so taken off guard, she gripped Penny's white wicker bedside table for support. After reminding herself that she didn't have to actually admit anything, she attempted to smile. Of course, she very likely failed and produced a sad imitation of one. "Where did that come from?" she asked lightly. "Wh . . . what made you think of your father?"

"All the other *kinner* at school talk about their fathers, but I never get to do that."

"We've talked about this before, dear. Not every family is made up of a mother and father. Sometimes—"

"I know, Mamm," her daughter said impatiently. "I know *Got* decides everything and He decided I didn't need a father."

Each word felt like more blows to her heart.

She had done this. She had fed her daughter lies and even brought their heavenly Father into it! She could practically feel her heart start to pound as she struggled to find the right words to end the conversation without making Penny upset. "You see, Pen—"

But her daughter talked right over her. "When I

told Mrs. Mast my *daed* was dead, she got sad and said that she was sure you missed him a lot. So, do you?"

"Well, I . . ." She swallowed. She supposed she should have realized that once Penny got to school she would start comparing her family to the other children's.

But now, after yesterday's conversation with Levi, she felt even more rattled. She was suddenly so tired of lying. So tired of making excuses to herself to explain the things she'd done.

"I'll go get your applesauce now, dear."

Penny groaned. "You didn't answer me, Mommy. Do you miss my daddy a lot?" Her eyes widened. "Or don't you? Are you glad he ain't here?"

Of course she was glad he wasn't there! Of course she didn't want him anywhere near her. She didn't want him anywhere near her precious girl!

But of course she couldn't say that.

Glancing at Penny, feeling the weight of her stare, Julia felt her brow begin to perspire. She clenched her hands into fists in a pitifully weak effort to control herself. When that did no good, she took a quick, calming breath. Then it was time to stop avoiding the inevitable. "I certainly wish you had a kind and loving father here," she said at last. "I have always wished that for you."

Penny leaned forward. Transparently soaking in every bit of information that she could.

Making Julia painfully aware that she'd rarely mentioned Luther to Penny at all. She'd never told Penny anything about him.

Instead, Julia had done her best to avoid any mention of Penny's father, hoping against hope that she'd be able to push away the inevitable conversation until she was at an age to understand why her mother had done the things she had.

But now Julia realized that had been a foolish hope. Of course, a child was going to want to know information about a parent. And, of course, Penny would have questions when she was confronted with the fact her home life was different than her other friends' situations.

As Penny gazed at Julia with hope in her eyes, Julia felt her throat close up and her mind go blank.

She didn't know how to tell Penny the truth.

This was worse than awful. When Penny realized that she wasn't going to share anything else, she leaned back against the headboard, then turned her head away.

Julia opened her mouth, then shut it quickly again. There was nothing to say. Turning around, she darted down the hall before Penny could point out that she had once again avoided answering her question.

The moment she entered the kitchen, she braced her hands on the counter and bowed her head. "Is this a test, Lord?" she whispered. "Are you showing me that once again I canna escape the past and that it was wrong of me to even try?"

When her eyes burned with even more unshed tears, she swiped at them impatiently. She needed to stop crying. Crying didn't help anything, and it surely had never helped her get anything done.

Turning away, she got out one of Penny's favorite bowls, a bright-pink plastic one that Julia had bought at a dollar store when she'd been just a baby. Now the bottom of the bowl was scratched from continued use and the edge was even a little torn up from when Penny had picked it up and decided it would be a perfect teething toy.

Examining it, she exhaled softly. "*Danke*, Jesus." That bowl was a nice reminder of all she'd already been through. Caring for a fussy, teething baby while living in a small motel room had not been easy. But she'd done it.

She'd worked long hours cleaning guest rooms with Penny by her side each day, then had somehow found the time and energy to play and read to her in the evenings. There had been many instances when she'd wanted nothing more than to lie down and rest, but she'd continued to push herself.

Those times had been difficult, too. But, again, she'd done it with the Lord's help.

This was yet another moment when she was going to need to remember that she wasn't alone in the world and she hadn't ever been. Not really.

Penny was her beautiful, glorious gift. Julia had never wished she hadn't gotten pregnant or that she'd had to raise Penny by herself.

Instead, having Penny had made her stronger, made her better. Made her world.

Julia wasn't perfect. Oh, no, she was far from that! But she was the best mother she knew how to be. And she'd been able to do that with God's help.

As she carefully spooned some applesauce that she'd canned herself the first week she'd moved into their rental house, Julia smiled. If Levi never forgave her for her lies, so be it.

If he decided to tell everyone in Charm that she wasn't a widow but rather an unwed mother, she would bear that, too.

As far as she was concerned, her lies hadn't hurt anyone but herself. She was still the same person that Levi knew. And if other people didn't want to know her because she'd made some mistakes six years ago, she could accept that.

She wasn't ready to share everything with Penny. She was too young to understand why her mother had done the things she'd done. But now Julia realized that one day she would tell her the truth. Penny deserved to know.

And one day soon, maybe even on Christmas Day, she'd place a call to her parents instead of simply writing them a letter. Though it was likely that they might have changed the number in the phone shanty, and probably wouldn't even go out to it to check messages for days, at least Julia would know that she had finally reached out.

"Mommy?"

"I'm on my way, child. I'm putting cinnamon sugar on your applesauce and getting you some water."

"Okay."

As she set everything on a tray, Julia had to smile at that. Okay. *Jah*, everything was going to be fine.

Looking up at the ceiling, she whispered, "*Danke, Got.*"

Chapter 23

❄ ❄ ❄

Really hoping he didn't look like a stalker, Levi stood at the window of his living room and stared at Julia's house.

About an hour ago, Julia had finally opened her front shades. He knew by now that she liked to enjoy the start of each day with the morning sun.

Just a few minutes ago he'd seen Julia walk into the room, then disappear to the back of the house, no doubt heading to the kitchen. She was probably getting coffee or breakfast, or something for Penny. Before long, she would be busy with household chores or stitching her quilt. She'd once told him that she enjoyed working on her quilts in the morning light.

Knowing all of that, Levi knew he couldn't procrastinate another minute. It was time to go across the street and apologize.

Somehow, some way, he was going to have to try to make amends. Even if she never forgave him for his harsh comments, he had to apologize. He couldn't bear to have her think that he was terribly cruel.

It wasn't like him, and it certainly wasn't fair to her.

Decision made, he went back to his own kitchen, which was still fairly clean, and he grabbed the cardboard container of cookies that he'd purchased from the café before he'd left work.

It wasn't much, but it was a peace offering. Well, that, and the puzzle and coloring book and fresh box of crayons he'd found at the fancy gift shop near the Carlisle Inn in Walnut Creek. He didn't know a lot about little girls, but he figured those two quiet activities might make Penny happy and allow her mother to get a little bit of rest.

After he slipped on his coat and stocking hat, he grabbed his gifts and strode across the street.

The sky was cloudy and gray. A northern wind was clipping along real good, too. They'd likely have a couple of inches of snow before nightfall. He made a mental note to shovel her driveway when he shoveled his own.

When he knocked, he heard her come to the door. He sensed that she was peering at him through the peephole. He kept himself still, letting her get a good look at him while she took the time to decide if she was going to let him into her home.

He didn't blame her hesitancy one bit.

When he heard the bolt unlock he was surprised at how relieved he felt. She was going to allow him to see her.

Thank the good Lord!

But when the door cracked open and he spied her face for the first time, he had to stop himself from stepping backward.

She looked ravaged, there was no other word for it. Her eyes were red and swollen, her cheeks looked blotchy, and there were new lines of stress creasing her brow.

"Hello, Levi. May I help you?" There wasn't a bit of warmth in her gaze.

He felt that cold regard all the way to his bones. "I hope so. May I come inside and speak with you?"

Her hand tightened around the door. "Now's not the best time."

Good manners meant he should accept her word and come back another time. Another day.

But he was afraid if he didn't push now, their relationship would only grow more distant. Gazing earnestly into her bruised eyes, he decided nothing would do but complete honesty. "Julia, please? I came to apologize."

Her hand gripped the door handle more firmly. "I don't think you need to come inside to do that."

Ouch. Feeling like everything that was between them was fading quickly, he started talking quickly. "I know you don't want to talk to me, and I don't blame you for not wanting to see me, either." He was speaking so fast, his words were practically tumbling over each other. "I know I said some terrible things the last time I was here. I didn't listen and I was judgmental."

"If you know all that, why do you expect me to give you another moment of my time?"

"Because you are a pretty special woman."

Her brows rose. "Now you think I'm pretty special?"

"I always have thought you were special." When she looked ready to interrupt him again, he blurted, "I know I don't deserve your time. But give it to me anyway."

"I'm so tired, Levi. I don't have the energy to do this—"

"I can help you. I could sit with Penny while you take a nap." When he saw her wavering, he lifted the sack in his arms.

"I brought gifts. Something for you and Penny." He didn't care that he sounded desperate. He felt desperate. He didn't want to lose what they had. Well, what he'd hoped they would one day have.

Ten seconds passed. Then twenty. He noticed then that she was wearing a dark-raspberry dress. It was pretty, and far more vibrant and cheery than the dark colors he usually caught sight of her in. He wondered if she'd chosen that color because she was planning to be home or if it was in honor of the holiday season.

No matter what the reason, he knew he liked seeing her in something cheerful. It made her look a little younger and a whole lot more carefree, as if she didn't have the weight of the world on her shoulders.

At last, she sighed in a way that told him her decisions had just about taken everything out of her. Stepping backward, she allowed him entrance. "I have a feeling I'm going to regret this. But come on in."

"I'm not going to let you regret this choice, Julia." He ignored the tightening of her lips and her wary expression. He was going to finally be the person she needed and could depend on.

After she closed the door, he took off his coat and hung it up on the hook by the door. "Where's Penny?"

"She is in bed."

"Is she awake? Can I see her?"

Her eyes clouded as she visibly pondered his question. He wondered what about it had caused her to hesitate. "I'd rather we talked first," she said at last.

"I understand." He bent down, loosened the laces on his boots, and slipped them off.

She stared at his boots like they were trespassers on her clean floor. "You are making yourself at home."

"Not entirely. I'm trying to be respectful of your clean *haus*."

She pursed her lips. "*Nee*, I don't think that's the whole reason." Crossing her arms over her chest, she glared. “As a matter of fact, I think you are being awfully heavy-handed, Levi.”

“I know you do.” And maybe she was right, too. Maybe he was being heavy-handed and a bit too pushy in order to worm his way back into her good graces. However, he figured he had nothing to lose. Crossing to the couch, he sat down and waited for her to do the same.

With obvious reluctance, she moved to sit across from him. Everything in her body language told him that she was unhappy about a great many things he was doing. “Go ahead and say whatever it was you came to say.”

Though he would have liked to ease into his explanation, he did as she asked. “Like I said, I feel badly about the things I said to you. I should have listened to you more. I should have thought more about what you had been going through. I am sorry, Julia. I hope you will forgive me.”

Staring at him, she nibbled her bottom lip. “I forgive you.”

It was their way to forgive. From her tone and the way she looked at him, he knew she’d been completely sincere as well. But he hadn’t thought she’d forgive him so quickly. “That’s it?”

“Well, something happened today that made me realize I’ve been a bit foolish to think that my past was never going to catch up with me. I should have known and been better prepared\ that I would need to confront it sooner than later.”

She sounded so sad, so reflective, he shelved the speech he'd mentally prepared and leaned forward, resting his elbows on his knees. "What happened?"

After glancing in the direction of her daughter's room, she lowered her voice. "For the first time that I can ever recall, Penny asked about her father this morning."

"What did she ask?"

"Nothing specific. She just asked about him. Asked if I missed him."

To Levi's surprise, he found himself waiting for that answer, too. "What did you say?"

She exhaled. "I'm not going to lie—her question took me off guard and threw me for a loop. At first, I couldn't think of anything to say."

"But then?"

"I told her that I did wish she had a kind and loving father." She smirked slightly. "So, I didn't actually lie. How was that for stepping around the truth?"

"Impressive."

"Hardly that. I felt frustrated with myself. And more than a little disappointed, too." Gazing at him directly, her light-brown eyes looking like melted toffee, she said, "I realize that I'm no longer going to be able to pretend that my past never existed and that my daughter will never have questions. It's difficult, but I'm coming to terms with that."

He supposed she was right. He had learned after he left town and went to Pinecraft that he should have handled things with his brother and Darla better. Running from problems didn't solve anything. Avoiding subjects only made future conversations harder. "What are you going to do about Penny's father now?"

"I don't want to contact him or anything," she said quickly. "She's too young now, of course, but . . . I think I am going to have to tell Penny the truth one day about me not really being a widow." She wrinkled her nose. "It's not going to be easy. I'm both dreading it and wishing it was already done."

"Perhaps the Lord will give you the right words."

"I can hope and pray for that." For the first time, there was a spark of humor in her eyes.

He was relieved to see that spark. He wanted her to be okay. He needed her to have some hope. Now he knew that he needed to help her, too. "Is there any chance that this man knows about her?"

"*Nee*," Julia said in a rush before a shadow fell over her face. "At least I don't think so. A couple of years ago I did tell my parents that I had a baby out of wedlock. I doubt they would have ever told Luther about her . . . but they might have. Or they might have told someone and it got back to him."

As much as he yearned to reassure her, he couldn't. "If I discovered that I had a daughter I never knew about, I would want to find her."

"If the situations were reversed, I would, too," she fairly whispered. "I know what I did wasn't right. But, Levi, some cuts are just too deep to heal. I honestly don't know how I would react if Luther came to find me."

"I have a feeling you might do better than you think. You are strong, Julia."

She swallowed. "I've wanted to be strong, but I haven't always been successful."

"You left Luther to protect your unborn child. You've made sacrifices in order to keep Penny safe. You stood up to me when I was being a jerk." Smiling softly, he murmured, "I think you might do better than you think."

"I hope so. Of course, I also hope I never have to find out."

Levi wished she was sitting by his side. He wished she trusted him enough to let him wrap an arm around her and hold her close. He wanted to comfort her, to do something to prove to her that she wasn't alone.

But because he couldn't, he did the next best thing. "I not only came over here to ask you to forgive me, I wanted to tell you that I now understand why you did what you did."

"Really?"

He nodded. "When you have something that

you treasure more than yourself, it is worth everything to protect it. A child is definitely one of those things."

"That's how I feel." Looking at her front door, she said, "In the middle of the night, I started thinking that maybe I didn't move far enough away. Maybe I should move to Indiana or Kentucky."

"*Nee.*"

"It may be for the best, Levi."

"It's not. You simply need a different plan." Before she could refute that, he blurted, "I meant what I said, Julia. I believe in you. I know you are strong . . . but what if you didn't have to face him alone?"

"It's not like I have a lot of people to reach out to."

"You don't need a lot of people. You only need one."

"What are you saying?"

Her voice had been hoarse. Almost filled with wonder. It broke his heart and made a lump form in his throat. It wasn't right that she felt so alone. It wasn't right that she'd been alone with no support system for years.

"I'm saying that you have me. You also have friends here. People who care about you. Julia, you have many people here in Charm who would never stand to one side and watch someone hurt you."

"I appreciate that, Levi, but I don't think you understand what he is like. He's a bully. He is going to want to be in Penny's life." Looking bleak, she added, "He's also not going to like that I pulled away from him for so long. He's going to either want to take Penny or, if I refuse or fight him, he'll force me to marry him. And what would you do if that happened? Do you think you could really stand in the way of that?"

"Yes. Of course I could." Right there, in that minute, Levi knew he spoke the truth. He was willing to do whatever it took, whatever he needed to do in order to make good on his promise.

She closed her eyes. "You don't know what he's like. I fear I wouldn't have much of a choice. If he forced me, threatened me with losing Penny, I fear I would do whatever he said."

He wondered what was going to happen if she ever saw Luther again. Part of him wondered if she made him up to be stronger and bigger and meaner in memory than he actually ever was.

Levi also wondered if she had really noticed his size. He wasn't a small man. He stood right at six feet and was strong from working with lumber all of his life. He didn't have the bulk of his older brother, but he certainly wasn't a man who could easily be cowed down or be unable to defend himself, if it came to that.

Quickly, he tried to think of the right way to

convince her, then decided there was only one way that she might believe in him. "You wouldn't have to worry about Luther forcing you to marry him if you already had a man in your life."

"What?"

"You heard me." A plan formed. It seemed so perfect, he was actually surprised he hadn't thought of it last night. "If you were married, you wouldn't have to worry about him appearing in your life ever again."

"What are you saying?" she whispered. She lowered her arms and waved them about. "Levi, you would marry me so I wouldn't have to fear him?"

"That's exactly what I'm saying."

She blinked, her honey-colored eyes flickering with doubt and shock. Her lips were parted slightly, almost as if she was at a loss for words.

Then she jumped to her feet. "This . . . that? It's ridiculous."

Two days ago, he might have agreed. But after their argument? After feeling the way he just had, even thinking about her moving away and him never seeing her again?

Now it sounded like a fine idea. A mighty fine one, at that. "Not so much. We were liking each other well enough before we fought," he retorted as he stood up as well. Needing to gain some weight in the conversation, he stepped closer. "Consider it, Julia. Don't say no."

"Don't say no? Do you . . . do you even hear yourself?"

"My hearing is fine." He stepped closer. "I'm thinking yours is, too."

"I don't know if it is or not, because I hear your words, but they're making no sense." She stepped toward him. "No sense at all."

"I think I'm making perfect sense. It's you who isn't listening to reason. And, for the record, I am not trying to force you to do something you don't want. I only want to help you."

"Asking me to marry for my safety or the safety of my daughter is most certainly not reasonable."

Before she asked him to leave, he said, "For the record, there are many advantages of marrying me." He grinned, not even caring if he sounded completely full of himself. "I'm a good man with a good job. My family is well-respected. Some women have even called me handsome."

"I just bet they have."

Grasping at anything he could think of to sway her, he said, "I should probably also mention that my family has money."

"I know that."

"Then you know if you married me, you would no longer be struggling to make ends meet. You could just take care of Penny."

She look at him searchingly. "I don't know what you want me to say," she said at last. "You already don't think much of the choices I've made. What kind of woman would I be if I took advantage of you in that way?"

"You wouldn't be taking advantage of me if I offered to marry you. Which I am doing."

"You are offering yourself to be trapped. Married to a woman who has so much baggage she can hardly carry it."

He knew what he needed to tell her. He needed to tell her his feelings. But because he was afraid of her rejection, he said instead, "I am stronger than I look, Julia. I can take your burdens."

"But I don't want to be taken care of."

"What do you want, then?"

She flinched. "I want what any other woman wants. I want what you are supposed to want, too, Levi Kinsinger. I want to be loved."

"I do love you," he blurted.

She gaped at him. "What did you say?"

"I love you." When she shook her head, he stepped closer. "I do." Feeling a little lightheaded, he said, "That is why I had such a difficult time when I realized you hadn't trusted me with the truth about your past. I have fallen in love with you and Penny, almost from the first time I met you both on this front stoop."

"I guess I'm not the only person who can lie," she said softly. Holding her hand out, she said, "Under the circumstances, I think it would be best if I simply passed on whatever you brought to Penny."

"You don't want me to see her?"

"I don't want her to think there's anything more between us than there is."

"Julia, I just said that you have my heart."

"How about this, then? I appreciate you coming over. I am grateful for the gifts for my daughter, and I am thankful that we talked." She cleared her throat. "I will also always remember how kind you were to offer to marry me. But I think, for right now at least, it would be best if we spent some time apart before we attempted to resume our friendship."

They were still practically standing nose to nose. He was close enough that he could smell the scent of fresh soap on her skin. He could see a smattering of freckles on her nose. He could see that there were flecks of gold in her irises.

He could even see her pulse beating in her neck.

And feel that it was not fear that was causing that. It was exactly the same thing he was feeling. A pull between them that had been evident from the very start.

Unable to stop himself, his gaze slid to her lips. They were slightly parted, her bottom lip was a little puffy, a little chapped. She'd been worrying it.

Then he knew what he was going to do. It wasn't smart and it wasn't wise. But he was as suddenly unable to stop his hands from raising to cup her shoulders as he was to stop anything, where she was concerned.

She inhaled sharply at his touch. “Levi.”

“I know,” he whispered as he bent his head down. “I know I shouldn’t. I know you shouldn’t let me.”

Then he gave her no time to answer because he was kissing her lightly on her lips.

Just once.

It was gentle. Sweet. Hardly more than a fast, fluid touch.

But it was still the sweetest kiss he’d ever experienced.

And by the look of wonder in her eyes, Levi was pretty sure Julia was thinking the same thing.

“Levi.”

“I know. But I would do it again, Julia. *Nee*, I want to do it again. Because I really do love you.” Letting his hands drift down her arms, he murmured, “One day soon I am going to hold you so close that you will feel only warmth. You will feel secure. You will feel like nothing and no one will ever be able to hurt or touch you without coming through me first.”

Her lips parted.

He pressed his lips to her cheek. Then moved to whisper in her ear. “And you will be glad I’m there, Julia. You will know that I will do anything in my power to keep you safe.” When she stiffened, letting him know that she was listening to every word he was saying, he curved a hand around her shoulders. "I will do anything to keep Penny safe. I will make you feel treasured and special and cared for. So much so, you won't ever want me to let go."

Abruptly, she pulled away. Her expression was panicked. Her eyes wary. "No one has ever talked to me like this."

"I know."

"I . . . I really don't know how to handle what you are saying," she continued, her voice hoarse. "I don't know how I'm supposed to respond."

"You don't have to say anything right now. But just let me tell you this. One day, if you keep me around, you will learn to expect all of these things from me, Julia."

She swallowed. "Levi. I, um, I think it would be best if you left now."

"I understand." He told her too much. He definitely shouldn't have kissed her. No doubt even Rebecca would have never been as bold as he had been.

"May I come back later today?"

"Today?"

"Please, to check on Penny?"

"*Jah.* Of course."

"*Danke.*" Just as he turned to leave, he remembered something else he had grabbed off his kitchen counter before coming over. He pulled out the pamphlet for The Refuge. "My friend Simon and his sister started this. It offers help for women and children who are in situations like you were in."

She took it hesitantly. "I saw this in your house when I cleaned."

"Did you read about it?"

"*Jah.*"

"I'm glad. Maybe you should think about stopping over there one day," he said, taking care to keep his voice easy. "Maybe when Penny is at school and you have some time on your hands."

"I don't know what I would do there. I'm not in that situation anymore. I got out."

"You did get out. But forgive me for saying it, but I'm starting to feel like you got your body out, but not your head." Realizing he had nothing to lose, he added, "You haven't moved on. You are still afraid of reaching out to your parents, you are still afraid to tell people the truth, and you are still lying about your identity."

"You now know my reasons."

"I do. And I completely understand your feelings and feel sorry for what you've had to go through as well. But I think there is a chance that you are still afraid, Julia. And is that how you intend to go through the rest of your life? Constantly looking over your shoulder on the off chance that Luther will appear in your life?"

"It is okay to be afraid of that."

"That is true. I want to help you. I want to give you my name and protect you, too. But I want you to feel like you are stronger as well."

"I'll think about it."

"*Danke.* Because if you don't, even if you never choose me, even if you never choose to love anyone, you need to come to terms with what has already happened. It's been my experience that the past always determines the future."

"Not always."

"Of course always. Because no matter where you are headed, it's right behind you, never all that far behind."

Grabbing his coat off the hook, he folded it over his arm as he stuffed each foot in a boot.

Then he walked out the door and down the steps, his untied laces lazily dragging on the ground.

For a moment, he paused, knowing that he needed to stop and tie them, but he didn't want to take the time. He would just have to make do.

Just like he was going to have to bide his time with Julia. For now, he'd pushed. He'd told her how he felt about her. He offered her some choices, both with him and something she could do on her own.

Now it was her turn. For better or worse, it was time for him to learn some patience.

He would do that, one step at a time.

• • •

Julia stood at the doorway, watching Levi stride across the street, moving as if he hadn't a care in the world. Even though she was becoming chilled, she couldn't seem to find the energy to move. She felt mentally exhausted and emotionally torn.

He'd surprised her. He was such a confident man, she hadn't ever thought that he'd be the kind of man to apologize or to explain himself.

His honesty had inspired her. His care for her and Penny had melted the ice around her heart a little bit, too.

She wasn't sure what was going to happen in her future or in their relationship. But she had been so struck by their conversation, she knew she wanted to think about it a little bit longer.

All that was why she was still standing in the doorway, watching him walk away.

She noticed then that his laces were trailing on the ground. With each step he took, she found herself giving into a little burst of apprehension, half expecting one of his laces to get caught on a twig or for him to inadvertently step on one and trip.

She would have never walked with loose laces. She would have taken the time to tie them, or maybe even wouldn't have taken them off in the first place so she wouldn't have to worry about putting them on again.

But not Levi. Like everything else that she'd

witnessed, Levi seemed impervious to something as mundane as tripping and falling.

Whimsically, she started thinking that those laces were a perfect metaphor for what he'd just said. They dragged and got dirty and threatened to trip him. To cause him harm. But, as she watched him enter his house without incident, she noticed that that little bit of problem wasn't causing him any delay or trouble. Instead of letting it bother him, he accepted that things weren't perfect and kept moving forward.

That was something she needed to learn to do one day. She was going to need to learn to accept her past, and instead of continually attempting to wish it hadn't happened or cover it up, she needed to come to terms with it and move on.

"Mommy?" Penny called out.

"Right here, dear." Still holding the presents that he'd brought, she walked into her daughter's room.

Penny met her gaze, then looked just beyond her. "I thought someone was here. It sounded like Mr. Levi. Was he here?"

"He was." Holding up the bag, she smiled. "He brought you a puzzle, a coloring book, and fresh crayons."

Penny smiled, but then continued to look concerned. "He didn't want to give them to me himself?"

"I asked him not to do that."

Hurt filled her gaze. "How come?"

"Well, I thought you might feel uncomfortable if he came into your room while you were in bed. Plus, you are still sick."

"Oh." She frowned. "I am sick, but I don't care if Levi comes to talk to me. I'd even talk to him if I was sitting in bed."

Of course Penny wouldn't have minded. Her daughter cared more about people than appearances. And she liked Levi. "I bet you'll see him another time." Trying to sound enthusiastic, she added, "Levi said he would stop by later today. You can see him then."

"Good."

"*Jah*. That is good. Now, what would you like to do? Do you want to color or work on the puzzle?"

"Will you do the puzzle with me?"

She had a lot of things to do, finishing up a quilt being the least of it. She was also exhausted. She also wanted to take another look at that brochure and do some thinking, just in case Levi was right and she did need to at last reach out and talk to someone about her past and the choices that she'd made.

But there was nothing more important than being with Penny. "Working on a puzzle sounds fun, dear," she said softly. "You put on a robe and slippers and I'll make us some hot tea. I'll meet you in the living room."

Penny looked delighted. "This is fun, Mommy. Now I'm glad I got a sick throat. Because of that, we can spend lots of time together."

Julia hugged her close. "You are exactly right, dear," she said. "Because of that, we can be together. Everything has a silver lining."

That was what she needed to keep in mind. No matter what, the only person she needed to keep focused on was standing right in front of her.

Chapter 24

❄ ❄ ❄

Tuesday, December 20

Penny was feeling much better in the morning. Her fever was gone and she woke up hungry for eggs and biscuits.

Though she didn't feel really good about her decision, Julia decided to take her with her on a quick trip to the market. There was no way she was going to leave Penny alone for that amount of time.

Penny, true to her usual form, was happy enough to go on a little trip to the store. Especially since Julia had told her she could take her teddy bear.

At the store, they walked down the aisles and got eggs and sausage and some baking powder. After picking up some apple juice, too, Julia guided her to the checkout counter.

"Hi, Julia! Hey, Penny!" Betty said with a smile.

"Hi, Betty," Penny said. "I've been sick but I'm getting better."

Betty looked at her sympathetically. "You had to run out for supplies, I see."

Julia nodded. "That's the good thing about living so close to the market. We can get the things we need without too much trouble."

"Hope you feel better, Penny," Betty said as Julia picked up her two bags full of groceries.

"*Danke.* Bye."

When they got outside, Penny held out her hand. "I'll help ya, Mommy. Give me a bag."

There on the sidewalk, they shuffled the bear, her purse, and the three canvas bags. After moving a couple of groceries out of one of the bags, Julia handed it to Penny. "Here you go, dear. Thank you for helping me."

Penny grinned up at her. "We've got to help each other, Mommy. Right?"

"That's right. We are a team of two," she said as she guided her down the street and through the busy crowd of last-minute holiday shoppers. "We are a perfect team of two. No matter what, we will always help each other as much as we can."

"May I help you?" a middle-aged Mennonite woman asked in a voice loud enough for everyone around them in the grocery store to overhear.

"I hope so," Luther replied. Holding up a ratty-looking teddy bear, he said, "I was unloading a shipment across the street when I noticed a little girl dropped her teddy bear as she and her mother were leaving this store. Her mother didn't notice and hurried her on before she could pick it up."

The clerk raised her eyebrows. "I didn't notice the mother and child. Didn't she buy anything?"

"I don't know. That wasn't my concern. I simply wanted to return the toy to her. You know how *kinner* like their playthings."

"That's real kind of you, mister, but I ain't got time to go track down any little girl to give her a teddy bear."

"Oh, I'm not asking you to do anything. I'll be happy to go give it to her."

Even though there was a line of four people behind him, she stared at him suspiciously. "Why would you want to go do that?"

Luther held his impatience in check and tried his best to look amiable. "I've been loading and unloading shipments nonstop all month. It would do my heart good to run such an errand."

But yet, she still looked doubtful.

"I saw it, too," an elderly woman said from behind him. "I was just wondering whether to call out to Julia when I saw you pick up Penny's bear." She laughed softly. "You might not believe this, but at first I thought you might be stealing that bear."

"I wouldn't do that. Just trying to be a good Samaritan."

At last the clerk smiled at him. "I'm sorry. I didn't mean to seem rude. What you're doing is mighty nice. Good luck finding Penny and Julia."

Penny. His daughter's name was Penny. "I saw them walking to the left. Any idea where I might run into them?"

The clerk looked doubtful again. "Well, I don't really know . . ."

But the other woman proved to be as helpful as ever. "I don't know where they were off to, but I know she lives nearby."

"I'm only trying to help. It is almost Christmas, you know," Luther said. "I imagine most any little girl would cry if she was without her favorite toy."

"Yeah." She frowned, no doubt wondering how much to reveal.

"If you could even tell me a general direction, I won't bother you anymore." He pressed.

"Excuse me, miss," another customer said impatiently. "I want my groceries in a canvas bag."

"Oh, sure." Looking more harried by the second, she blew a batch of bangs away from her forehead. "Sir, Julia usually heads home. She's renting a house up on Jupiter Street."

"I'll head in that direction. Thank you."

"Not a problem. Merry Christmas."

"*Jah*, you too." He smiled at her, then headed back outside. Walked in the direction Julia had been pulling his daughter, glancing at the street signs as he quickened his pace.

He passed one street. Then the next. Then, there it was. Jupiter Street. Feeling stronger than he had in some time, he paused to catch his breath, then turned up the street.

Now all he had to do was discover which house she lived in.

It wasn't going to be hard. He had a name. He could do anything. Because nothing and no one was going to prevent him from getting his daughter back.

"So that's where we are now," Levi said to Lukas, Rebecca, Rebecca's husband; Jacob, and Simon.

The four of them stared at him in concern, then exchanged glances with each other. Levi wished he could read their minds. Had he shocked them? Disappointed them?

"That's quite a story you got there," Jacob said at last.

"I know. I don't know what to do now."

When he'd arrived at work that morning, Lukas had taken one look at his face and called an impromptu gathering in his office.

Levi hadn't considered protesting even a little bit. The truth was that he had no idea what to do next with Julia and Penny. He needed all the advice he could get. He didn't even care that they were using company time to talk.

The moment they'd understood that he needed them, his brother, brothers-in-law, and Rebecca had sat down and told him to start talking.

And so he did. He'd shared everything he felt he could. Now that that was done, he felt a little worn out, like he'd just completed a long race and needed to replenish and rejuvenate.

"Here's what I think," Rebecca said. "You need to keep going back and talking to Julia."

Lukas shook his head. "She might not want to listen. I think one of us ought to go over there and help Julia see reason."

Imagining that scenario, Levi shook his head. "She's not going to be real anxious for you to tell her what to do, brother. Actually, I don't think she's going to even let you in the door."

"I could go," Rebecca volunteered.

"Or I could go with Amelia," Simon said. "Julia will trust Amelia, and I can talk to her about The Refuge and Tess."

"I like that idea," Jacob said. "No offense, Rebecca, but I think Simon and Amelia might have the right touch."

"None taken. What really matters, Levi, is that you don't give up on Julia. She needs you."

There was something in the way she said that that took him off guard. "You hardly know her. Why would you say that?"

"It's the way you look when you talk about her. It's different. You're different."

"Different, how?"

"Different like she means something to ya," Lukas replied. "Different like you are willing to do more for her."

It was on the tip of his tongue to refute that. He was no different than he'd ever been. But as he thought about how she was always on his mind, how he had been willing to call off work to help her and Penny, how he had been eager to introduce her to his siblings, to risk upsetting her because he wanted her to feel safe and secure, to even risk making her mad at him because her happiness meant more to him than his own, he knew Lukas was right.

"I guess you have a point." Looking out toward the horizon, he said, "I didn't expect this to happen. I came home because I was worried about Amelia and to get back to work. I didn't come back from Pinecraft in order to fall in love."

Wait a minute. Had he just admitted that he was in love to his family?

Their laughter told him everything he needed to know.

"Glad you could join us, brother," Simon said. "We were wondering if you were ever going to give love a try."

"*Danke.*"

Lukas stood up. "Ordinarily, I would say we really needed to get back to work, but it's a slow day around here. Simon, why don't you and Levi go talk to Amelia and then head over to Julia's."

"Hold on, now," Levi protested. "We've got shipments coming in. And Peter was counting on me to help him learn to file."

"I can help him do that," Jacob said.

"And Marcus Mast can monitor the trucks arriving," Lukas added. "It will all get done."

"It always does," Rebecca said with a winsome smile. "I'll pray for you and Julia. And for Simon and Amelia, too. I don't know why, but I have a feeling something big is about to happen."

"I think that's called Christmas."

"Of course it is. But what I'm thinking of is something more."

Simon walked toward the door, "Come on, brother. Let's go find my fiancée and solve your problems."

Levi almost told him to stop calling him brother, but then he held his tongue. It was turning out that he needed Simon as much as he needed any of his siblings.

Matter of fact, it was becoming apparent that he might need as many people reaching out helping hands as possible.

Chapter 25

❄ ❄ ❄

"*Danke* for bringing over the vegetable soup, Jane," Julia said as she walked her neighbor out onto the front porch. "It was a nice surprise."

"I was happy to help. We neighbors need to look out for each other, you know."

This was just what she'd hoped for all those months and years when she worked at the motel in Millersburg. She'd wanted to have a normal, easy life filled with hard work, a home to go to sleep in at night, and friends and a community for both she and Penny. Jane's arrival proved to her that such a thing really was possible.

And after all the difficult conversations she'd been having with Levi, Jane's gesture meant the world to her.

"Lately, it feels like you are doing all the looking out for me. I hope one day soon I'll be able to do something for you."

Jane waved her off. "Don't worry about that. Good neighbors and good friends don't keep tally. We are simply there for each other whenever we can be."

"I'll remember that. *Danke.*"

Jane took another step down the porch. "I better

get on back. There's no telling what's happening at my house right now. My father came over to watch my *kinner*, and he seems to think that means letting them do whatever they want."

"I heard that it is a grandfather's job to give their grandchildren their heart's desire."

Jane grinned. "If that is the case, my *daed* is a mighty *gut dawdi*, indeed. See you soon."

"*Jah.* See you soon!" she replied—just as she noticed a man standing at the bottom of her driveway.

Right then and there, her body felt as if it had turned to ice.

"Hello, Julia."

Luther. Panic engulfed her. Stepping backward, she reached for the door handle. Maybe she would be able to go inside and lock the door?

"Don't do it, Julia," he said as he walked up the driveway. "We have much to talk about. Too much to talk about for you to even think about running."

Her hands started shaking. Everything inside of her warred with her body's reaction. She knew she should run. She knew she should call out to Jane's retreating form and ask for help.

She knew she should talk back to him, say something, say anything.

But it was as if her body was incapable of listening to reason. Instead of doing anything that was right, she remained where she was, half frozen, silently watching him walk toward her as if he had all the time in the world and as if he knew she was no challenge to him.

As he approached, she noticed that he looked much the same. His dark-brown hair was a little longer, there were more lines around his eyes and mouth, Maybe he'd gained eight or ten pounds.

But his piercing glare was the same. The anger that radiated from him was also familiar. Too familiar.

He stopped at the base of her porch stairs. "Where is she?"

Her mouth went dry. "Who?"

"Don't play games with me. Where is my daughter, who you hid from me for five years?"

"She is inside."

He walked up the stairs, energy and anger radiating from every muscle. "I need to see her."

Seeing his face, hearing the rough tone of his voice, and picturing how frightened Penny would be of him spurred her into action. She needed to be strong and above all else, she needed to protect Penny at all costs.

"*Nee*, Luther," she said. "I will not allow you near her."

"What did you say?"

"You heard me. She's been sick and I will not have her frightened with you barging in like this."

"I have every right to see my daughter. And we both know that your time of being her mother is drawing to a close."

“I know no such thing.”

He looked so incredulous at the way she was talking back to him, it was almost laughable. After staring at her for almost a full minute, he shook his head and gripped her arm. “*Nee*, Julia.”

His fingers dug into her arm, pulling her skin, making her wince in pain. When she’d been engaged to him, she used to pretend his pain didn’t affect her. She used to pretend that her bruises didn’t come from his fingers. She used to pretend that her body wasn’t sore from his callous treatment.

Now, however, she had no such qualms. She cried out and jerked her arm from his grip. His hand went slack, before he pushed her against the wall of the house.

Her shoulder hit first, then her elbow. “Luther, you must—”

“No, Julia,” he bit out as he slapped her hard. “No more.” Looking almost icy calm, he pulled open the front door and walked inside.

Walked inside the first home she’d ever made for her and Penny. Inside the first safe place she’d found for the two of them. But the walls and plaster had proved to be as much of an illusion as the sense of security she’d felt.

It was fleeting, fragile, and, in the end, a mirage.

Later, Julia would wonder how she’d got to her feet and raced inside mere seconds after him. But as she scrambled through the house toward

Penny's room, she could only tell that her heart was pounding and her breaths were shallow. Her face hurt from where he'd struck her, and her arms already felt bruised.

But none of that mattered. "Penny!" she called out. "Penny!"

"Mommy?" Penny's voice was high-pitched and trembling.

"I'm right here," she said as she rushed into Penny's room. Her mouth went dry as she saw that Luther was standing by Penny's bedside, a combined look of shock and hesitancy on his face.

"She looks like you," he said. "She has your blond hair and your brown eyes."

Julia didn't know if he was stating a fact or offering a criticism. "Yes, she does," she said quietly as she edged closer to her daughter's side.

"Mommy?" Penny whispered as she tried to shrink away from Luther's imposing presence. Obviously, she was confused and frightened. "Mommy, who is he?"

The innocent question seemed to force him out of his stupor. He abruptly turned to Julia, and once again his expression turned irate. "Are you going to tell her, Julia, or shall I?"

"Mommy, who is he?"

She almost lied to them both. She almost fabricated a story that Penny was another man's child. It almost sounded like a good idea. Especially since she knew she'd still do anything,

anything to remove him from her daughter's side.

But she was done lying. And, it seemed, she was done avoiding her past as well. Quietly, quickly, she asked the Lord to give her the strength she needed to protect her daughter. And, perhaps, to bear the pain that was sure to occur no matter what ever happened in the future.

"Penny, this is your father." Just as Penny shook her head and seemed ready to protest, Julia hastened to explain. "I know I told you he was dead, but that wasn't true. I, well . . . I told you a lie."

"Why?" Penny asked.

"Because he hurt me," she said with brutal honesty. "Because he hurt me and I was afraid that he would one day hurt you."

Luther's expression was thunderous. "You will regret this."

"I already do." But regrets only took up empty space in her heart and didn't help her handle the future. Softening her voice, she said, "Penny, don't worry. Nothing is going to happen."

Tears filled her daughter's eyes, and they broke her heart. "I know it's hard. One day I will be able to explain it all to you."

Before Penny could respond, Luther said, "Get her dressed. We're leaving."

"Where would we go?"

"I'm taking you back to Middlefield. Where you belong."

"I belong here. And so does Penny."

Just as he drew back a hand to strike her again, a knock sounded at the door.

"Julia?" a voice called out. It sounded loud and confident. It sounded like Levi.

"Don't speak," Luther warned.

Another day, another time in her life, she wouldn't have said a word. She wouldn't have risked his anger. But now she had so much more to lose.

She also knew that Levi was someone who she could trust. She didn't need to be saved, but she certainly did need some help.

With that in mind, she did the only thing she could do. She breathed in deep, opened her mouth, and screamed.

Chapter 26

Levi had never heard a sound that could reverberate through his insides and cause such a stark amount of extreme pain as when he heard Julia's cry.

Exchanging a look with Simon, they opened the door and ran inside. Amelia was on their heels until Simon stopped abruptly, turned, and placed his hands on her arms.

"Stay right by the door, Amy," he said.

"I want to join you. I want to help."

"You know I won't be able to do anything if I am worrying about you, and I'm always going to worry about you first."

"You're right. Go."

"Levi!" Julia called out. It was followed by another sharp cry and a sound of Penny crying.

Levi raced down the hall.

When he entered Penny's room, a man about his height, but at least thirty pounds heavier, blocked his way. "Leave. This ain't no business of yours."

Levi looked beyond him, seeing Penny openly weeping and Julia attempting to calm her through tears of her own.

"Julia, are you hurt?" he asked loudly. "Has he hurt you?"

"I think I'm okay," she replied. Her voice was shaky.

Studying her, Levi noticed that she had a red mark on her face and her arms were protectively wrapped around her middle. She was shaken up and scared. She wasn't okay at all.

When Simon appeared behind him, the man blocking the door looked far more concerned.

Levi didn't blame him. Levi looked as Amish as could be. He was strong, but he had nothing on Simon. Simon had participated in illegal fighting for several years after he left Charm. He'd also been in prison for a period of time. And though he was firmly entrenched in the Amish way of life, he had no fear of violence.

"Move," Simon said. "Move or I will make you move."

The man glared at Simon, opened his mouth to say something, then met his eyes and seemed to think better of his choice. He took two steps backward, not far, but giving Levi and Simon enough room to push their way inside.

"Don't go anywhere," Levi practically growled to Luther. "We are not done."

As Luther looked fully prepared to argue that point, Simon said, "Levi, take care of things here."

Simon stayed next to Luther as Levi strode over to Julia sitting on the side of the bed, Penny in her arms, hiding her face. Tears were falling down her cheeks . . . and continued to break his heart.

"I . . . I don't know how you knew to get here, but I'm so glad you did."

"Me, too," he murmured as he reached out and ran his fingers over her face, taking care not to hurt her bruised cheek any further.

Sitting down on the mattress next to them, he pulled her and Penny into his arms. "You poor girls. I am so sorry."

"I'm scared," Penny whispered.

"I know. But you don't have to be anymore. I'm here. And Simon is, too."

Both were trembling against him. He wanted to do nothing more than whisper that he'd solve all of their problems. That he'd make everything better. But he knew that it was too early to say such things.

Little by little, Penny's tears abated and Julia looked better, as if she had gathered herself together.

To his surprise, Luther and Simon were quiet. Simon looked like he had all the patience in the world to hold Luther at bay, and Luther seemed more than a little stunned that Julia and Penny were not alone with him.

After reassuring himself that they were all right, though definitely a little bruised and battered, he joined Simon at the doorway.

"You need to go," he said simply. He didn't

want to fight, he only wanted this man out of Julia's house and away from her child. He figured after he got them away, he would have plenty of time to walk with Julia to the police so she could make a statement.

But Levi's words spurred a new resolve in Luther's eyes. "I ain't going anywhere. You canna keep me away from my child." Glaring at Julia, he added, "Not anymore."

Levi didn't want to give him any concessions, but he also realized that the man had a point. "I agree, but this isn't the way to see her. You canna force your way in here, hurt Julia, and attempt to kidnap her and her daughter. You need to go through the proper channels."

"Levi?" Julia asked.

"It's okay, Julia," he murmured. "You are not alone anymore."

Luther glared. "What are you talking about? I have no need for others to get involved."

"You do, just like we all do."

Luther's eyes darted back to Penny. "Not anymore."

Simon stared hard at him, seemed to come to a decision, then said, "Amelia, come here for a moment, will ya?"

When she appeared in the doorway, he said, "Go see Tess. She's dating that cop. Tell her what's going on. She'll contact him and take care of the rest."

Without a word, Amelia walked out.

Luther looked ready to explode. "What are you doing?" he asked as Simon's grip on him tightened. "You're going to get the Englishers involved?"

"We've got no choice," Levi said. "You hurt Julia. You were going to force them to go with you. None of that is okay."

Actually, it was all so much worse. As the reality of what had occurred resonated inside of him, as he imagined what could have happened, that Luther could have harmed Julia worse or taken both of them away from Charm, away from him, Levi's anger ignited.

"I've never wanted to harm another person in my life, until this very minute," he said in a quiet, firm tone. "Julia has told me how you treated her, how you abused her. The things you threatened. And now, here you are without a shred of remorse?"

"I have nothing to be sorry for."

Just as Simon was about to join in, to Levi's surprise Julia jumped to her feet.

"You have done nothing?" She shook her head. "You have done everything! It was because of you that I had to leave. I have lost so much for these last six years."

"You have our child." Peering over at Penny, he said, "I am your father. You should have been with me from the beginning. But you will. I promise, you are never going to be apart from me ever again."

Penny's eyes were wide with fright. She kept staring at him but looked also like she was trying to burrow against her mother. "Mommy, I don't want to."

If there was ever a thing that seemed to break the camel's back, it was that statement. With a cry, Luther pulled away from Simon's grip, and rushed toward the bed.

Suddenly, everything felt as if it was happening in slow motion. Penny screamed, Simon rushed forward, Julia shielded her daughter's body with her own, and Levi did something that until that moment he'd been sure he would have never done.

He grabbed Luther's shirt, pulled back his right hand, and hit him on the chin as hard as he could.

Instantly, Luther fell to the ground. Unconscious.

Simon grinned. "I didn't know you had that in ya."

Rubbing a hand over his face, Levi tried to regain his composure. "I . . . well, honestly, I didn't think I did. I never wanted to resort to violence, either."

"You didn't have a choice."

Maybe he had. Maybe a smarter, better man could have resolved the situation in a calmer fashion. But Levi knew he wasn't that person.

Hesitantly, he said, "It seems the Lord knew that I needed Him and gave me the strength to do what was necessary. Though He might be disappointed in me, I can only give Him praise."

"Amen," Simon said—just as the front door opened and Amelia, Tess, and two police officers came in.

Chapter 27

Julia wasn't sure if she'd ever been surrounded by so many people who cared about her at one time. After the police questioned her, called for an EMT, and debated for the space of a minute whether to charge Levi with anything, they took Luther away.

One of the medical doctors who had helped Luther examined Julia and then assured Levi that she hadn't sustained any worse injuries than a couple of bad bruises and a black eye. After the doctor recommended that she rest for a few days, and Amelia and Levi promised him that Julia would be taking it easy, the doctor left.

Soon after, people from all over Charm started arriving. Mrs. Crane brought a pitcher of spiced cider. Angel came over from work, bringing a basket of cookies with her.

Next came Jane with her husband by her side. Tess and Lukas and Darla and Rebecca and her husband, Jacob, walked in her door moments later.

Somehow, they encouraged her to settle on the couch in a fresh dress and to put her feet up. They arranged a finely crocheted afghan around her and fussed after Penny, too.

Darla's sister Patsy arrived with Maisie and Gretel and a bucket of cute wooden farm animals. Though Penny looked tired and still a bit skittish, Julia knew that her little girl was relieved to put the afternoon's events behind her for a while.

The three girls were now in Penny's room, having a small party since Patsy had given permission for them to have both hot chocolate and a plate of Christmas cookies in her room.

Seeing everyone crowded around her and hearing voices in the kitchen, where Patsy and Rebecca were heating up the lasagna that they'd brought, made Julia feel secure and happy. However, it was Levi who she was most appreciative of.

Through it all, he'd stayed by her side. He brought her hot tea, put cool compresses on her eye, and even held her hand—right in front of everyone. She was ever so grateful.

After all, she'd been alone for so long. She'd been full of doubt about the choices she'd made in life and scared of everything coming to light. She'd carried those burdens for so very long. But now she didn't have to worry about that anymore. Her secret was out and her biggest fears had come true. Luther had found her and discovered Penny.

But she and Penny had survived.

And though only God knew what was going to happen next, she realized that whatever did happen was going to be all right. She had survived.

"You've been pretty quiet," Levi said. "You hanging in there?"

"*Jah.*" Looking at him, and at Tess, Simon, and Amelia, who were either sitting on the couch or on the floor, she said, "I was just sitting here thinking that both my worst fears and greatest wishes happened all in one day. It's a little hard to take in."

"That man was scary," Amelia said. "I would have run from him, too."

Simon reached out to wrap a reassuring arm around her shoulders. "You did a good job getting help, Amy."

Julia smiled to herself. Simon was so tough, and had been so ferocious, it now was more than a little amusing to see how tender he was with Amelia.

"I am sorry I lied to you all," she said. "I know it wasn't right, but I didn't know what else to do."

"Of course you didn't," Angel said. "From what everyone is saying, that man didn't fight fair or believe in rules. If he didn't, then you couldn't fight him by following the rules, either."

Julia hadn't thought about it that way, but she figured Angel had a good point. "I am sure we'll be talking about what happened for some time. Just, thank you for still being my friends."

To her surprise, everyone chuckled instead of looking touched.

"What did I say?"

Tess reached out, took her hand, and patted it. "You are getting things kind of backward, Julia. You don't need to thank us for being your friends. We are simply glad we are."

"She's right, you know," Levi said softly. "Don't ever thank me again for caring about you. I want to look after you for the rest of my life."

"I won't, then. I promise."

After another hour, her guests started to trickle out. It had started snowing again, something that all the children were excited about, seeing as Christmas was in just a couple more days.

After promising to stop by in the morning with an egg casserole and fresh biscuits for breakfast, Jane and her husband left. Angel went next, with Julia's quilt in her arms.

"Wait, Angel," she called out. "I'm not done with it."

"I know that. We're going to have a quilting party at the shop tomorrow," she said brightly. "Four ladies are going to come in to help me finish it."

"This close to Christmas? This is your busiest week of the year! I couldn't let you do that."

"That's *gut*, because I didn't ask your permission. We're finishing this quilt, dear, because I know of an Englisher who would just happen to love to buy a beautiful Amish-made quilt that was white-on-white for Christmas. You'll get your money!"

Julia's cheeks heated. She wasn't entirely happy to have her secret told so bluntly to everyone in the room, but she didn't say a word about that. After all, she'd just been through something far worse than a little bit of embarrassment about her finances.

"Darla and I are going to walk you home," Lukas called out to Angel. "Don't you step one foot out the door without us."

Darla winked in Julia's direction. "He's bossy, but his heart is in the right place."

Twenty or so minutes after that, Patsy walked out of Penny's bedroom with Maisie and Gretel. She reported back that the toys were neatly put away, Penny's face was washed, and she was sleeping peacefully in her bed. Then she left with Rebecca and Jacob.

After promising to stop by the following day, Simon and Amelia and Tess left, too. Leaving Julia and Levi alone at last.

After Levi stood up and locked the door, he returned to her side. "I didn't think they were ever going to leave," he teased.

"Are you going to stay a while?" She really hoped so.

"*Jah.* I'm going to sleep here on the couch tonight."

"That isn't necessary. I'll be fine."

"It is for me. If I stayed across the street, I fear I wouldn't do anything but stand in front of my window and look over here." He shook his head. "I don't think I'll ever be able to fully describe what it felt like to hear your scream and then to see you and Penny alone and afraid with that man. I tell ya, my heart felt like it was in my throat."

"I'm so glad you came."

He stood up. "Me, too. Now, what can I get you? Some tea? More supper?"

"I don't need anything. Just your company."

"Well, I can give you that." He smiled again.

"Are we going to be all right?" she finally asked tentatively. "Do you think you will ever truly forgive me for lying to you?"

"That isn't even a worry. Do you think you will ever be able to forgive me for not trusting you and taking care of your faith in me?"

"That isn't even a worry."

"*Gut.*" He smiled at her. As the seconds passed, he opened his mouth like he was about to say something but didn't.

"What is it?" she finally asked.

"I want to know two things."

"Ask whatever you want."

"First, will you come over to my house for Christmas dinner?"

"*Jah.* I think I can make it across the way. I'll make something, too."

"*Nee*, not that little place. My house. My family's *haus*."

His big house where his heart was. Where his whole family was going to be. "Are you sure you want me and Penny there?"

"You know I do. I'm going to want you there a whole lot in the future, too, Julia. I'm going to want you to live there with me one day."

Even though she'd been sure that she couldn't cry any more tears, she felt her eyes fill again. "I would like that," she said simply. She didn't need him to explain more, or to give her a declaration of love. Not right now. Based on what had happened today, she knew he cared deeply for her. Just as she cared for him.

Levi had brought in his family, his help, and his confidence into her life. He loved her, too. And because of that, he'd made her realize that her future was going to be bright, indeed.

"I'd like that," she said again, with a smile.

"There's that dimple I like so much," he murmured, just before he bent close and pressed his lips to her brow.

"Levi, I'm fairly sure the kettle is still hot. Would you please pour me a cup of tea?"

He got to his feet. "I'll get it. And I'll get a second helping of lasagna for me and even bring you a reindeer cookie or two. We'll sit and talk and eat and then get some sleep. Okay?"

"It sounds perfect."

Better than even her dreams.

Chapter 28

❄ ❄ ❄

Christmas Day

Christmas had come again.

Looking around his family home's massive living room, with the big stone fireplace, fine-looking wood floors, and multiple couches and chairs, Levi Kinsinger knew that nowhere else would feel as perfect.

This was the place where he'd crawled on the floor and his father had, too. This was the place where he'd chased Lukas, argued with Rebecca, and played with Amelia.

It was the place where his mother had smiled and told every one of them to settle down and act like the *kinner* she'd raised.

And it was also the place where he'd sat and mourned her death. His father's, too.

After each change, he'd been sure that nothing would be the same. He'd been sure that this house wouldn't feel like home. Of course, he had been both right and wrong. Nothing ever stayed the same and everything always changed. Both, it seemed, were inevitable, at least for the Kinsinger family.

Now, as he watched Darla's siblings laugh about some story Jacob had told and listened to the women laugh in the kitchen, Levi knew that years from now, their children would be taking over things and perhaps doing exactly what he was doing . . . being pleased and grateful for his family and his many blessings.

"You look like a mighty happy man, Levi," Lukas said as he plopped down in a chair next to him. "Care to share the reason?"

He shrugged. "I was just sitting here, watching the *kinner* and listening to the women and thinking about how everything changes yet stays the same, too."

Lukas grinned. "I've often thought the same thing. When Daed died, I was sure all of us could never fill his shoes."

"And we haven't."

"But we've done well enough. Ain't so?" Stretching his feet out in front of him, he shook his head in wonder. "It may take four of us to do it, but we've managed to continue to run the mill. We even had a better year than last year."

"That's because of you, not me. I took off to Florida."

"You did. But you came back. That's what counts. One day, I'll be taking Darla on a vacation for a month and you can hold down the fort."

"I'll be glad to do it. Just tell me when."

"Will do."

"What are you two talking about so earnestly?" Rebecca asked as she walked closer with Amelia.

"Change and constants."

"Like us," Amelia said, looking a bit delighted. "The more we stay the same, the more we change, too. Especially this year." Looking across the room at Simon, who was sitting with his brother, Jeremy, his sister, Tess, and her foster mother, Jill, she sighed. "I love our mixed-up, perfectly imperfect family."

"Me, too," Rebecca commented, smiling at her husband, his parents, and her stepdaughter, Lilly. "All of us have found love this year." She paused. "I can't believe that what I was sure was going to be the hardest year has also been the best."

"You are certainly happier with Jacob."

"I am." Looking at the three of them, Rebecca said, "I think I could say the same of all of you." Smirking, she said, "Even Levi now."

Maybe if everything hadn't happened, Levi would have flushed or been completely embarrassed. Instead, he couldn't help but agree. "You're right. I met Julia and Penny, right where I least expected it."

"Does this mean you're finally going to move out of that crummy house?"

"It does."

Lukas's eyes lit up. "Does it mean you'll be

moving back with your new wife and step-daughter, too?"

"Hopefully. I told Julia that was my hope."

All three of his siblings sat up. "You told her?" Rebecca asked excitedly. "Does that mean you are engaged now?"

"Not yet. I have a bit more work to do to get her to say yes to marry me. But I think I might be able to convince her sooner than later."

Amelia tilted her head to one side. "I'm thinking it might be much sooner than later," she said softly. "Look at them now!"

Levi hadn't realized she'd come into the room, too. Standing up, he scanned the area, then let himself simply enjoy the sight of Julia and Penny sitting on the thick rug in front of the fireplace.

Julia was wearing a yellow dress. It was an unusual shade for the winter, but it suited her perfectly. Against the firelight, it looked almost gold. It set off her pretty hair and made her golden-brown eyes look the color of caramel.

But what was the most mesmerizing was the fact that she was smiling while she talked to Penny. Her dimples looked adorable.

She looked adorable, as did Penny. Penny was in a bright Christmas-red dress and playing with the set of wooden farm animals Patsy and Maisie had brought her a few days ago. Next to her was a fancy baby doll in a fluffy dress.

"I'm going to go sit with them," he told his siblings.

Lukas stood up. "*Jah*, I should probably pull Darla out of the kitchen and sit with her, too."

Seeing Simon walk toward Amelia, Levi decided they would all be in comfortable pairs before too much longer.

Julia looked up and smiled when he approached. "Hiya, Levi. Penny and I were just playing with her farm animals."

"I saw that." Crouching down, he turned to Penny. "May I sit with you?"

Penny nodded as she held up a little goat. "The goats are talking about climbing on the stones around the fireplace."

"It looks as good a place as any. Not as good as a barn at Hershberger's, but it is close. Later, if you want, we'll go out to the barn and say hello to Princess, Amelia's pet goat."

"I thought Princess came inside sometimes. Didn't she come into the *haus* for Thanksgiving?"

"She did, but that didn't go too well. Even Amelia came to that conclusion."

Penny giggled.

As she started putting the four goats on the fireplace, Levi bent closer to Julia. "She seems better today."

Julia nodded. "She is. We went over to The Refuge yesterday."

"Did you talk to anyone?"

"Not any social workers or anything. But we sat and talked to Tess and her brother Jeremy. To my surprise, Penny talked to Tess a lot. She still doesn't completely understand everything that happened, but I think she does understand that Luther wasn't a good person, and she is glad she isn't going to have to see him again anytime soon. And Officer Perry came in and told me that charges were filed against Luther. It was enough to keep him in jail until he could post bail."

"Good. When he gets out, we'll work out the next steps."

"*Jah.* Tess told me that I'm going to have to get a lawyer, but she would help me find one. And Jeremy told us that we should come by on Saturday afternoons sometimes. I guess some other single women with children are going to start meeting there, just so they could have time to talk."

"All that sounds good, but I don't want you to go there for long."

"Why?"

"The single mom club. I want you to be at the happily married mom club."

She laughed. "That one will be a joy to join, for sure and for certain."

Just as Levi was about to respond to that, Lukas tapped a spoon against one of the glasses.

"Hey, everyone, can I have your attention, please?" he asked.

It took a while, but all of them gathered into the room and faced Lukas. When everyone's attention was on him, Lukas looked a little bit uncomfortable, but cleared his throat.

"It just occurred to me that we are all together. We've prayed, we've exchanged small gifts, and we've both eaten and cleaned up an enormous meal. But we haven't done one important thing."

"What's that, Lukas?" Lilly asked.

"We haven't exactly taken a moment to remember what today is all about."

"It's Christmas, Luke," Rebecca teased. "We haven't forgotten that."

"Of course not, but I had something else in mind." When everyone quieted again, Lukas took a deep breath and gazed at them all around the room. "To me, when I think of Christmas, I don't think of holly or presents or snow or even sparkling lights and cookies. Christmas, to me, is all about Jesus's birth. And having hope and having faith. It's about new beginnings, whether it's a babe in the manger or four siblings who were a little lost but somehow found themselves again."

Looking around the room, he smiled. "And right at this minute? To me, Christmas is about family and love."

"It is about family and love," Jill said. "I couldn't agree more."

Lukas grinned as he held up his glass. "So,

here's to that, everyone. Here's to Jesus and hope and new beginnings and family . . . but most of all, love. And because every person in this room means all of those things to us, Christmas is you, too. Merry Christmas."

"Merry Christmas," everyone called out right back, some with tears in their eyes.

As several people raised glasses and hugged, Levi let his gaze linger around the room. Noticed the smiles and the jokes and the chatter.

The room couldn't have been more warm or happy or bright.

It was everything he'd always remembered and hoped it would one day be again.

Lukas had been exactly right. It was Christmas.